AN ADAPTED CLASSIC

Little Women

Louisa May Alcott

GLOBE FEARON
Pearson Learning Group

Adapter: Emily Hutchinson
Project Editor: Kristen Shepos-Salvatore
Editorial Supervisor: Sandra Widener
Editorial Assistant: Kathleen Kennedy
Production Editor: Alan Dalgleish
Marketing Manager: Sandra Hutchison
Art Supervision: Patricia Smythe
Electronic Page Production: Luc Van Meerbeek
Cover and Interior Illustrator: Laurie Harden

ISBN 0-8359-1866-1
Printed in the United States of America

12 13 14 15 V013 15 14 13

1-800-321-3106
www.pearsonlearning.com

CONTENTS

ABOUT THE AUTHOR

Louisa May Alcott (1832-1888) was born in Germantown, Pennsylvania. When she was two years old, her family moved to Boston. Her father, Bronson Alcott, founded the Temple School there. In this school, he put his ideas about childhood education into practice. He thought teachers should help children develop their minds, bodies, and spirits. Alcott also thought children should be able to express themselves freely.

Bronson Alcott's school closed within six years. After that, the family moved to Concord, Massachusetts. There, Louisa's father started a farm and a vegetarian community. Neither of these earned much money. Alcott could not support the family.

Soon, Louisa's writing became the main income for the Alcotts. For some years, she wrote short stories for magazines and newspapers, just as the character Jo did in *Little Women*.

In 1862, during the Civil War, Louisa became a volunteer nurse in a military hospital. She soon became ill, and her health was ruined. But she had plenty of material for the work that made her fame as a serious writer. Her *Hospital Sketches* (1863) was based on her work in the hospital.

Louisa May Alcott was a strong backer of women's rights. The women in her novels succeed in medicine, acting, and painting. Her support of these ideas, however, never weakened her belief in self-sacrifice, moral purity, and devotion to husband and children.

PREFACE

The March family in *Little Women* is based on the author's own family. The character of Jo is based on Louisa herself. Jo looks and acts very much like Louisa May Alcott. Louisa's sisters, Anna, Elizabeth, and May, were the models for Jo's sisters in the book.

Little Women first appeared as a magazine series. It was published as a book in 1868. It was the first American children's novel to become a classic. Even though it is thought of as a novel written for young people, the book has always been popular with adults as well. More than 100 years after the author's death, all of her novels for young people are still in print.

Little Women, the most famous of her novels, is available in more than 25 editions. Over the past 60 years, it has been made into four different movies.

ADAPTER'S NOTE

In preparing this edition of *Little Women,* we have kept as closely as possible to Louisa May Alcott's original words. We have changed some of the vocabulary. We have also shortened and combined some chapters.

Some of the footnotes explain difficult words. Other footnotes give historical detail. We have tried to keep as much of the author's original style as possible as we adapted her most famous work.

HISTORICAL BACKGROUND

The family into which Louisa May Alcott was born was well known in the United States. Her father, Bronson Alcott, was a leading figure in the transcendentalist movement. This movement reached its height in New England during the 1840s. At that time, Louisa was not yet an adult, but the movement influenced her for the rest of her life.

According to transcendentalism, the mind is most important. A person's feelings are the best guide to truth. This movement stood for self-expression. Its followers were taught to seek the truth wherever they might find it.

The movement helped develop several American ideas. These include the importance of the individual, self-reliance, and the idea that races and sexes should be equal. Transcendentalists also thought that people and the natural world depended on each other for survival. These ideas continue to be important in our own time. They certainly play a part in *Little Women*.

CHARACTERS

JO

Second-oldest of the four March sisters. Her main talent is in writing.

MEG

Oldest of the four March sisters. She remembers when the family had more money, and longs to be rich so she can enjoy the finer things.

BETH

Third-oldest of the four March sisters. She is never happier than when she is playing the piano and singing.

AMY

Youngest of the four March sisters. She is very skilled in social situations, and deeply wants to belong to the best society.

MARMEE

Mother of the four March sisters. She is always ready with a moral lesson to guide her daughters.

FATHER

Head of the March family. He is serving as a chaplain during the Civil War.

LAURIE

March family's next-door neighbor. He is about the same age as Jo, and he is friends with the March sisters.

MR. LAURENCE

Laurie's grandfather. He was a good friend of Marmee's father.

MR. BHAER

Also known as "Professor Bhaer" and "Fritz." He befriends Jo in New York.

JOHN BROOKE

Laurie's tutor. He falls in love with Meg.

HANNAH

Servant in the March household. She is thought of as a friend and member of the family.

AUNT MARCH
 Father's rich aunt. She is an old, weak woman who needs the daily help of a young person.

AUNT CARROL
 Another aunt. She takes Amy with her to Europe.

1 *Christmas, 1860*

"Christmas won't be Christmas without any presents," grumbled Jo, lying on the rug.

"It's so dreadful to be poor!" sighed Meg, looking down at her old dress.

"I don't think it's fair for some girls to have so much, and other girls so little," added little Amy.

"We've got Father and Mother and each other," said Beth contentedly from her corner.

"We haven't got Father, and shall not have him for a long time," said Jo.

Nobody spoke for a minute. Then Meg said, "You know why Mother suggested not having any presents this Christmas. She thinks we shouldn't spend money for pleasure when our men are suffering so in the army."[1]

"I think we could each spend one dollar on ourselves. I want to buy a new book for myself," said Jo, who was a bookworm.

"I want some new music," said Beth, sighing.

"I need some new drawing pencils," said Amy.

"Let's each buy one thing. I'm sure we've worked hard enough to earn it," said Jo, looking at the heels of her shoes in a gentlemanly manner.

"I know *I* have, teaching those tiresome children nearly all day when I'd rather be home," said Meg.

"You don't have half the problems I do," said Jo. "How would you like to be shut up for hours with a fussy old lady who is never satisfied with anything?"

---

1. This story is set during the time of the Civil War, and Mr. March is with the Union army.

"I do think washing dishes is the worst work in the world," said Beth, sighing loudly.

"None of you suffer as I do," cried Amy. "You don't go to school with mean girls who laugh at your dresses and label your father if he isn't rich."

"You must mean *libel,*"[2] laughed Jo. "Don't talk about *labels,* as if Papa was a pickle bottle."

"Don't you wish we had the money Papa lost when we were little, Jo?" asked Meg, who could remember better times.

"Well, we still are a pretty jolly set," said Jo, and she began to whistle.

"Don't, Jo. It's so boyish!" said Amy.

"That's why I do it."

"I detest rude, unladylike girls!"

"Really, girls, stop fighting," said Meg. "And, Josephine, you are old enough to stop acting like a boy. Remember, you are a young lady."

"I'm not! I hate to think that I've got to grow up and be Miss March, and wear long gowns, and look prim and proper! It's bad enough to be a girl, anyway, when I like boys' games and work and manners so much better! I can't get over my disappointment in not being a boy. It's worse than ever now, for I'm dying to go and fight with Papa, and I can only stay at home and knit, like a poky old woman!"

"Poor Jo! It's too bad, but it can't be helped. Try to be contented with making your name boyish, and playing brother to us girls," said Beth.

"As for you, Amy," continued Meg, "you are altogether too prim and proper."

Because young readers like to know how people

2. **libel**   to say or write something that damages a person's reputation

look, we will take this moment to give them a little sketch of the four sisters. Margaret, who was nicknamed Meg, was the eldest of the four. She was 16 years old and very pretty, with large eyes, soft brown hair, a sweet mouth, and white hands, of which she was rather vain. Jo was 15 and very tall and thin. She reminded one of a colt, for her limbs always seemed to be in her way. Her long, thick hair was her one beauty, but it was usually up in a net, to be out of her way. Beth was a rosy, smooth-haired, bright-eyed girl of 13. She had a shy manner, a timid voice, and a peaceful expression. Amy, though the youngest, was a most important person—in her own opinion, at least. A regular snow-maiden, with blue eyes, and curly yellow hair, pale and slender, she always acted like a young lady mindful of her manners.

The clock struck six, and the girls started getting ready for Marmee's return. Beth put her mother's slippers near the fireplace to warm them. Meg lighted the lamp. Amy got out of the easy chair without being asked, and Jo held the slippers nearer to the blaze. As they did this, Beth suggested that they spend their money on gifts for Marmee instead of for themselves. The others agreed.

"We must go shopping tomorrow afternoon. Tonight, we really have to rehearse our play for Christmas night," said Jo. "Come here, Amy, and do the fainting scene. You're not very good at it yet."

"I can't help it. I never saw anyone faint."

"Do it this way: Put your hand on your forehead. Then stagger across the room, crying frantically, 'Roderigo! Save me! Save me!'" Jo let out a truly thrilling scream.

Amy tried to copy Jo, but she just couldn't get it right. Jo groaned, and Meg laughed out loud.

"Glad to find you so merry, my girls," said a cheery voice at the door. The girls turned to welcome Marmee, who was, in their opinion, the most splendid mother in the world.

"I've got a treat for you," she said. A quick, bright smile went round the room like a streak of sunshine.

"A letter! A letter! Three cheers for Father!" cried Jo.

"I think it was so good of Father to go as chaplain when he was too old to be drafted and not strong enough to be a soldier," said Meg, warmly.

"When will he come home, Marmee?" asked Beth.

"Not for many months, dear, unless he is sick. Now come and hear the letter."

They all drew to the fire, Marmee in the big chair and the girls gathered around. It was a cheerful, hopeful letter, full of lively descriptions of camp life, marches, and military news. At the end, the writer's heart overflowed with love and longing for his girls at home.

"Give them all my dear love and a kiss. I know they will be loving children to you and perform their duties well, so that when I come home, I may be fonder and prouder than ever of my little women."

Everybody sniffed when they came to that part. Jo wasn't ashamed of the great tear that dropped off the end of her nose. Amy sobbed, "I *am* a selfish girl! But I'll try to be better, so Father won't be disappointed in me."

"We all will!" cried Meg. "I think too much of my looks, and I hate to work. But I'll change, if I can."

"I'll try to be what he calls me, 'a little woman,' and not be so rough and wild," said Jo.

Beth said nothing, but she resolved in her quiet little soul to be all that Father wanted her to be.

Mrs. March broke the silence by saying, "Everyone

longs for goodness and happiness. That longing guides us through many troubles to find true peace. And I know my girls will do their best."

For the rest of the evening they sat in the living room, sewing. At nine they stopped work and sang as usual, before they went to bed.

Jo was the first to wake on Christmas Day. She woke her sisters, and they went down to the kitchen.

"Where is Mother?" asked Meg.

"Goodness only knows. Some poor creature came begging, and your ma went straight off to see what was needed. There never *was* such a woman for giving away food and drink, clothes and firewood," said Hannah, who had lived with the family since Meg was born. They all considered her more of a friend than a servant.

"She'll be back soon," said Meg. Just then, steps sounded in the hall.

When Marmee walked in, she said, "Merry Christmas, little daughters! I want to say one word before we sit down. Not far away from here lies a poor woman with a little newborn baby. Six children are huddled into one bed to keep from freezing, for they have no fire. They have nothing to eat, and the oldest boy came to tell me they were suffering from hunger and cold. My girls, will you give the poor Hummel family your breakfast as a Christmas gift?"

They were all very hungry, and for a minute no one spoke. But almost immediately, they started packing up the meal. Then the procession set out. Soon they got to the poor, bare room. Some of the windows were broken, and there was no fire. A sick mother, a crying baby, and a group of pale, hungry children all cuddled under one old quilt, trying to keep warm.

In a few minutes it seemed as if kind spirits had

been at work there. Hannah carried wood and made a fire. She closed up the broken window panes with her old hats and her own cloak. Mrs. March gave the mother tea and cereal, and comforted her with promises of help. She dressed the little baby as tenderly as if it had been her own. The girls, meantime, fed the children like so many hungry birds, laughing and talking the whole time.

The girls thought that it was a very happy breakfast, even though they didn't get any of it. That morning, no one was merrier than the hungry little girls who had bread and milk on Christmas.

"That's loving our neighbor better than ourselves, and I like it," said Meg. While their mother was upstairs collecting clothes for the poor family, the girls set out their presents for her. There was a great deal of love wrapped up in those four little bundles.

"She's coming! Three cheers for Marmee!" cried Jo, prancing about, as Meg escorted Mother to the seat of honor. Mrs. March was both surprised and touched. She smiled with her eyes full of tears as she opened her gifts. There was much laughing and kissing and explaining. It is what makes these home festivals so pleasant at the time, and so sweet to remember later.

The rest of the day was spent preparing for the evening festivities, the performance of a play written by Jo. After the play, there was a wonderful surprise waiting for the girls—ice cream, cake, fruit, and bonbons. There were also four great bouquets of flowers.

"This is from old Mr. Laurence," said Mrs. March.

"The Laurence boy's grandfather? What put such a thing into his head? We don't know him!" said Meg.

"Hannah told one of his servants about your breakfast party. He is an odd old gentleman, but that pleased him. So you have a little feast at night to make up for the bread-and-milk breakfast."

"That boy put it into his head, I know he did! I wish we could meet him. He looks as if he'd like to know us, but he's bashful," said Jo.

"I should have asked him in when he brought the flowers. He looked so sad as he left, hearing all the fun upstairs and having none of his own," said Marmee.

"We'll have another play sometime. Perhaps he'll help act. Wouldn't that be jolly?" said Jo.

"I never saw such beautiful flowers," said Meg.

Beth nestled up to Marmee and said softly, "I wish I could send my bunch to Father. I'm afraid he isn't having such a merry Christmas as we are."

A few days after Christmas, Meg and Jo received an invitation to a New Year's Eve party at the Gardiners' home. The only party dress that Jo owned had a small burn in the back. Meg told her she would have to sit still as much as possible, and keep her back out of sight.

For the party, Meg wanted a few curls around her face, and Jo tried to help by pinching her hair with a pair of hot tongs. When she removed the curling paper, the hair came with it. Jo timidly laid a row of little scorched bundles on the bureau before her victim.

"What *have* you done? It's ruined! I can't go! My hair, oh, my hair!" wailed Meg, looking with despair at the uneven frizz on her forehead.

"I'm so sorry, but the tongs were too hot, and so I've made a mess," groaned poor Jo.

"Tie your ribbon so that the ends come on to your forehead a bit. It will look like the latest fashion. I've seen many girls do it like that," said Amy.

Finally, the girls were ready, and even though Meg's high-heeled shoes were too tight, she would not say so.

Dear me, let us be elegant or die!

"Have a good time, girls!" said Marmee, as they left the house. As the gate closed behind them, she called, "Have you both got nice handkerchiefs?"

"Yes, yes, very nice. Meg has cologne on hers," cried Jo. Then she said to Meg, "I believe Marmee would ask about our handkerchiefs if we were all running from an earthquake."

"Well, a real lady is always known by neat boots, gloves, and handkerchief," replied Meg.

When they got to the Gardiners', they were greeted kindly. Meg knew Sallie and was at ease very soon. But Jo, who didn't care much for girls or girlish gossip, stood with her back carefully against the wall. She felt out of place. She could not roam about the room, for the burned spot on her dress would show. When the dancing began, Meg was asked at once. She smiled so much that no one would have guessed how much the tight shoes were hurting her feet.

Jo saw a tall boy headed her way. Fearing that he would ask her to dance, she slipped into a curtained side room, planning to watch the party from there. Unfortunately, another bashful person had chosen the same place. As the curtain fell behind her, she found herself face to face with "the Laurence boy."

"How are you this evening, Miss March?" he asked.

"Very well, thank you, Mr. Laurence, but I am not Miss March, I'm only Jo," she said.

"I'm not Mr. Laurence, only Laurie."

"Laurie Laurence—what an odd name!"

"My first name is Theodore, but the fellows called me Dora. I made them say Laurie instead."

"I hate my name, too. I wish everyone would say Jo, instead of Josephine."

Jo and Laurie continued to talk in the side room. Jo

found that she liked "the Laurence boy" very much. They would have talked for hours longer but Meg sprained her ankle while dancing in the tight high heels and had to go home early. Luckily, Laurie's grandfather had sent a carriage for him. They all got into it, and Meg was saved the pain of walking home.

Beth and Amy were waiting up, eager to hear all about the party. Jo had saved some bonbons for the little girls, and they enjoyed those while hearing the most thrilling events of the evening.

Over the next few weeks, Meg found her thoughts dwelling on the days before her father had lost his property in trying to help a friend. She wished her life was still as easy as it had been then. All around her she saw young ladies who had more party dresses, bouquets, and other nicer things than she would ever have. Now, instead of going to theaters, concerts, and sleighing parties, Meg worked as a governess, bringing her small salary home. She was beginning to feel that it wasn't quite fair. She had not yet learned how rich she was in the blessings which alone can make life happy.

Jo spent her days as a companion to Aunt March, who was weak and needed an active person to wait on her. One of the reasons Jo enjoyed her position was the large library of fine books at Aunt March's house. Since Uncle March had died, the books had been left to dust and spiders. Now, with Jo in the house, all that changed. As soon as Aunt March took a nap or had company, Jo hurried to the library, curled up in the easy chair, and read poetry, history, and travel books.

Beth was too shy to go to school. She had tried it, but she suffered so much that it was given up. She did her lessons at home and helped Hannah do the housework. By nature she was a busy bee. Beth loved music, and she tried very hard to learn, although she couldn't take music lessons or have a fine piano.

Amy had a great talent for drawing, and was never so happy as when copying flowers, designing fairies, or illustrating stories. She could also crochet, play twelve tunes, and read a little French.

Each girl had her own talents, her own wishes, and her own reasons for being unhappy. Marmee listened to the girls and sympathized with them, but she knew that they would soon learn that riches can not buy happiness.

2 Getting to Know Laurie

One winter afternoon, Jo went outside, a broom in one hand and a shovel in the other, to dig paths around the house. The snow was light. With her broom she soon swept a path all around the garden. The garden separated the March house from the Laurences' house. On Jo's side of the hedge was her family's brown house, looking rather bare and shabby, robbed of its summer vines and flowers. On the other side was the Laurences' stately stone mansion. Yet it seemed a lonely house, for no children played there and no motherly face ever smiled through the windows. Few people went in and out, except the old gentleman and his grandson.

To Jo, this fine house seemed a kind of enchanted palace, full of delights that no one enjoyed. She wanted to get to know "the Laurence boy" better. On this snowy afternoon, Jo decided to do something. She saw Mr. Laurence drive off, dug her way through the snow down to the hedge, and looked over. She saw a curly black head leaning on a thin hand at the upper window.

"There he is," thought Jo, "poor boy! All alone on this dismal day. I'll toss up a snowball and make him look out and then say a kind word to him."

Up went a handful of soft snow. The head turned at once. The big eyes brightened and the mouth smiled. Jo called out, "How do you do? Are you sick?"

Laurie opened the window and called out, "Better, thank you. I've had a bad cold for a week."

"I'm sorry. What do you amuse yourself with?"

"Nothing. It's dull as tombs up here."

"Have someone come and see you then."

"I don't know anyone."

"You know us," laughed Jo.

"So I do! Will you come, please?" cried Laurie.

"I'll come if Mother will let me. I'll go ask her."

Five minutes later, Jo rang the bell at the Laurence house. She was let in by a servant and brought up to see Laurie. She had a covered dish in one hand and Beth's three kittens in the other.

"Here I am, bag and baggage," she said. "Mother sent her love, and Meg sent some of her blancmange.[1] Beth thought her cats would be comforting." Beth's loan turned out to be just the thing, for while he laughed over the kittens, Laurie forgot his shyness.

Soon Jo was telling Laurie lively stories about Aunt March. She described the fidgety old lady, her fat poodle, the parrot that talked in Spanish, and the library. When she told him about the prim old gentleman who came to visit Aunt March and how the parrot had tweaked his wig off, Laurie lay back and laughed till the tears ran down his cheeks. Then they talked about Jo's sisters, their plays and their plans, and, of course, books. To Jo's delight, she found out that Laurie loved books as much as she did, and had read even more than she had.

Laurie then took Jo on a tour of the house, stopping at last at the library, which was even better than Aunt March's. Jo was invited to stay for tea. It was then that Mr. Laurence saw the change in his grandson. As Jo and Laurie chatted away like old friends, there was

---

1. **blancmange** a sweet dessert made from milk that has been boiled and thickened with cornstarch or gelatin, flavored, and cooled in a mold

color, light, and life in the boy's face.

"I hope you'll come again," Mr. Laurence told Jo.

After tea, Jo and Laurie went for a walk in the conservatory.² It seemed quite wonderful to Jo. She went up and down the walks enjoying the flowers, the soft light, the damp sweet air, and the wonderful vines and trees. Laurie cut the finest flowers, saying, "Please give these to your mother. Tell her I like the medicine she sent me very much."

When Jo got home, she told her sisters every detail about the visit. "That was a nice little speech about the medicine Mother sent him," Meg said.

"He meant the blancmange, I suppose."

"No, Jo! He meant *you,* of course! You don't know a compliment when you get one," said Meg.

"I think compliments are a lot of nonsense, and I'll thank you not to be silly and spoil my fun. I like Laurie, and I won't have any stuff about compliments and such rubbish. We'll all be good to him, because his mother and father are dead. He can come and visit, can't he, Marmee?"

"Yes, Jo, Laurie is very welcome," said Marmee.

Over the next few weeks, the girls got to know Laurie quite well. At first, they felt strange because they were poor and Laurie was rich. But after a while, they could see that Laurie was grateful to know them. The new friendship grew like grass in spring. Never having known a mother or sisters, Laurie found the girls very interesting. Their lively ways made him ashamed of the lazy life he led.

What good times they had together! They put on plays that had been written by Jo. They went sleigh-

---

2. **conservatory** a greenhouse or glass-enclosed room for growing and displaying flowers and other plants

riding and ice-skating. Now and then they had charming little parties at the great house. Meg could walk in the conservatory whenever she liked. Jo read for hours at a time in the library. Amy copied pictures, and enjoyed beauty to her heart's content. But Beth, though longing for the grand piano, was too shy to go over to the house and use it. Mr. Laurence, learning how shy Beth was, found a way to get her to come.

One day, when he was sure Beth could hear him, he said to Mrs. March, "The piano suffers from not being used. Wouldn't some of your girls like to run over, and practice on it now and then, just to keep it in tune? They wouldn't have to see or speak to anyone at all. I'm in my study at the other end of the house. Laurie is out a great deal, and the servants are never near the piano after nine o'clock."

Beth decided to speak. "I'll come, if you are sure nobody will hear me—and be disturbed." She trembled at her own boldness as she spoke.

"Not a soul, my dear. The house is empty half the day. Come and play the piano as much as you like, and I shall be obliged to you."

"How kind you are, sir!" said Beth, blushing like a rose. The next day, after seeing Mr. Laurence and Laurie leave, Beth went through the side door. She made her way, as noiselessly as any mouse, to the drawing room, where the piano stood. Quite by accident, of course, some pretty, easy music lay on the piano. With trembling fingers, Beth touched the great instrument. Right away she forgot her fear and everything else but the wonderful delight that the music gave her. The songs were like the voice of a beloved friend.

After that, she slipped through the hedge every day. The great drawing room was haunted by a tuneful spirit that came and went unseen. She never knew that Mr. Laurence often opened his study door to hear her play the old-fashioned tunes he liked so well. She never saw Laurie stand in the hall, warning the servants to stay away. She never suspected that the new song books she found were put there for her.

To show her thanks to Mr. Laurence, she knitted him a pair of slippers. Two days after she left the slippers in his study, he sent her a wonderful gift, along with a thank-you note. The gift was a little cabinet piano. The note explained that it had once belonged to the granddaughter he had lost.

"Beth, that's an honor to be proud of! Laurie told me how fond Mr. Laurence used to be of the child who died, and how he kept her things. Just think, he's given you her piano!" said Jo.

Beth tried it, and everyone said it was the most remarkable sounding piano ever. It had been newly tuned and put in apple-pie order. But its real charm lay in the happy faces that leaned over it, as Beth lovingly touched the beautiful keys and pressed the pedals.

A few days later, Amy was looking out the window as Laurie rode by on his horse. "I wish I had a little of the money Laurie spends on that horse," she sighed.

"Why?" asked Meg.

"I'm dreadfully in debt," said Amy.

"In debt, Amy? What do you mean?" asked Meg.

"Why, I owe at least a dozen pickled limes. The girls are always buying them. Everyone sucks on them during class. At recess, everyone trades them for pencils, bead rings, paper dolls, and other things. If one girl likes another, she gives her a lime. They treat by turns. I've had ever so many. But I haven't been able to return them, and I should. They are debts of honor, you know."

"How much money do you need?" asked Meg, taking out her purse.

"A quarter would be enough."

"Here's the money," said Meg.

The next day Amy bought 24 limes on the way to school. The rumor went through the room that she was going to treat the other girls. Unfortunately, Mr. Davis, the teacher, found out about it. He had just set a new rule against having limes in the classroom, putting limes in the same category as chewing gum, novels, and newspapers.

Mr. Davis had taken his coffee too strong that morning, and there was an east wind, which always affected his mood. In the language of the schoolgirls, "He was as nervous as a witch and as cross as a bear." The word "limes" was like fire to gunpowder. He rapped on his desk to get the attention of the girls. Then he said, "Miss March, come to the front of the room. And bring with you the limes in your desk."

Mr. Davis forced Amy to throw all the limes out the window. Then he told her to hold out her hand. Too proud to cry or beg, Amy did as he said. Mr. Davis then rapped her little palms several times with a ruler. He did not hit her hard, but that made no difference to her. For the first time in her life, she had been struck. The disgrace, in her eyes, was terrible.

"You will now stand in front of the class until recess," he said. That was dreadful. It would have been bad enough to go to her seat and see the pitying faces of her friends, or the satisfied ones of her few enemies. To stand in front of the class caused Amy a shame and pain that she never forgot. To some, it might seem like nothing, but Amy had known only love for the 12 years of her life. A blow of this sort had never touched her before.

The 15 minutes until recess seemed like forever to Amy. As soon as she was dismissed, Amy ran home. After being told the whole story, Mrs. March said, "I don't approve of corporal punishment, especially for girls. I dislike Mr. Davis's manner of teaching. You may study at home with Beth, and I shall ask your father's advice before I send you to another school."

"I wish all the girls would leave and spoil his old school. It's perfectly maddening to think of those lovely limes," sighed Amy, with an injured air.

"I'm not sorry you lost them. You deserved some punishment for breaking the rules," said Marmee. This surprised Amy, who had expected nothing but sympathy.

One Saturday not long after this, Jo and Meg were invited by Laurie to a play. Amy wanted to go too, and said she would pay for her own ticket. "You can't come, Amy," said Jo. "You wouldn't be able to sit with us. Our seats are reserved. You could not sit alone, so Laurie would give you his place, and that would spoil our plans. You'll just have to stay home."

Amy began to cry when Laurie came. As they were leaving, Amy called down, "You'll be sorry, Jo March!"

Jo, Meg, and Laurie had a charming time, for the play was as wonderful as the heart could wish. When they got home, they found Amy reading in the parlor. She didn't ask one question about the play. Jo began to think that she had forgotten her anger. There, Jo was mistaken. The next day she made a terrible discovery. The book she had been writing was gone. Amy finally admitted that she had burned it. "You wicked, wicked girl! I'll never forgive you as long as I live!" cried Jo.

When Mrs. March came home and heard the story, she soon brought Amy to a sense of the wrong she had done. Jo's book was the pride of her heart. It was only half a dozen little fairy tales, but Jo had worked them over patiently for several years. She had put her whole heart into her work, hoping to write something good enough to print. Jo looked so grim that it took all Amy's courage to say meekly, "Please forgive me, Jo. I'm very sorry."

"I never shall forgive you," was Jo's stern answer. From that moment, she ignored Amy. That evening, as Jo received her good-night kiss, Mrs. Marsh whispered gently, "My dear, don't let the sun go down upon your anger."

Jo was so deeply injured that she really *couldn't* forgive Amy yet. "It was a terrible thing, and she doesn't deserve to be forgiven," replied Jo.

The next day, Jo asked Laurie to go skating. Amy watched her leave, wishing that Jo had invited her, too, for it was the last ice of the year. "Go after them," said Meg. "Don't say anything until Jo has gotten good-natured with Laurie. Then take a quiet minute, and just kiss her, or do some kind thing. I'm sure she'll be friends again, with all her heart."

"I'll try," said Amy, and she got her skates and ran after Jo and Laurie, who were just disappearing over the hill. It was not far to the river, but Laurie and Jo were ready to skate before Amy reached them. Jo saw her coming, and turned her back. Laurie did not see her, for he was carefully skating along the shore checking for thin ice.

"I'll go on to the first bend, and see if it's all right, before we begin to race," said Laurie.

Amy struggled to put her skates on, and Jo went slowly zigzagging down the river after Laurie. As Laurie turned the bend, he shouted back, "Keep near the shore. It's not safe in the middle."

Jo heard, but Amy was just struggling to her feet, and did not catch a word. Jo glanced over her shoulder, thinking to herself, "No matter whether she heard or not. Let her take care of herself."

Moments later, Jo heard the ice crack. Then she heard a splash and a cry that made her heart stand still with fear. She tried to call Laurie, but her voice was gone. She tried to rush forward, but her feet had no strength. For a moment, she could only stand motionless, staring with a terror-stricken face at the little blue hood above the black water. Then Laurie's voice cried out, "Bring a rail. Quick!"

How she did it, Jo never knew, but she dragged a rail from the fence while Laurie stretched out on the ice and held Amy up by his arm. Together, they managed to get the child out of the icy river. Shivering, dripping, and crying, they got Amy home. She finally fell asleep, rolled in blankets, before a hot fire.

"Are you sure she is safe?" whispered Jo.

"Quite safe, dear. She is not hurt. You were so sensible to bring her home quickly," said her mother.

"Laurie did it all. Mother, if she *should* die, it would be my fault." Then Jo told her mother all that had happened, sobbing out her gratitude that Amy was safe. "It's my dreadful temper! I can't control it. Oh, Mother, what shall I do?" cried Jo, in despair.

"You must keep trying. You think your temper is the worst in the world, but mine was just like it."

"Yours, Marmee? Why, you are never angry!"

"I've been trying to cure it for 40 years, and I have only succeeded in controlling it. I feel anger nearly every day of my life, Jo, but I have learned not to show it. When I feel angry, I just go away a minute and try to get it under control. Your father is the best example for me. He never loses patience, never doubts or complains."

Just then, Amy stirred in her sleep. Jo looked at her sister and said, "I let the sun go down on my anger. I wouldn't forgive her. Today, if it hadn't been for Laurie, it might have been too late! How could I be so wicked?" Jo leaned over her sister, softly stroking the wet hair scattered on the pillow.

As if she heard, Amy opened her eyes and held out her arms. Her smile went straight to Jo's heart. Neither said a word, but they hugged each other close, in spite of the blankets. Everything was forgiven and forgotten in one loving kiss.

3 From Spring to Summer

"I do think it was most fortunate that those children got the measles. This way, I don't have to work for a while. I can accept Annie Moffat's invitation for a whole fortnight[1] of fun," said Meg, as she packed her trunk.

"I wish I could go, too," said Amy.

"I wish you all were going, but since you can't, I'll tell you everything when I get back. Now, let me see, I have the new gray suit and the old party dress. My bonnet isn't as nice as Sallie's, and my umbrella is not as pretty as Annie's. I wonder if I shall ever be rich enough to have real lace on my clothes, and bows on my caps?" said Meg.

"You said the other day that you'd be happy if you could only go to Annie Moffat's," said Beth in her quiet way.

"So I did! Well, I *am* happy, and I won't complain. But it does seem as if the more one gets, the more one wants, doesn't it?" said Meg, as she finished packing.

The next day Meg left, in style, for a fortnight of pleasure. Mrs. March had agreed to the visit rather reluctantly. She feared that Meg would come back more discontented than when she went. But Meg had begged so much that Marmee gave in. So, off Meg went to taste fashionable life.

After a few days, Meg began to envy Annie Moffat. Home now seemed more dismal and work seemed harder than ever. She longed to be rich. When the evening for the "small party" came, Meg found that

---

1. **fortnight** two weeks (from fourteen nights)

her dress was not really good enough. But then the maid brought in a box of flowers, and the note on them said they were from Laurie to Meg. By the time she had made up a few little bouquets for the hair and dresses of herself and her friends, she was feeling better.

Meg was having a wonderful time at the party, until she overheard some of the guests talking about her. "Poor thing! She'd be so pretty if she only had more stylish clothes. Do you think she'd be offended if we offered to lend her a dress for Thursday?" said one voice.

"She's proud, but I don't think she'd mind. That dowdy dress is all she has. She may tear it tonight. That would be a good excuse for offering a decent one," said another.

Meg *was* proud, and her pride was useful just then. It helped hide her shame and anger at what she had just heard. She was glad when the party was over, and she was quiet in her bed, where she could think.

Poor Meg had a restless night, and got up half ashamed of herself for not speaking out to her friends. That morning, Annie told Meg that she had invited Laurie for Thursday, and asked her what dress she would wear.

"My old white one again, if I can mend it. It got sadly torn last night," said Meg. She tried to speak quite easily but felt very uncomfortable.

"I have a lovely blue silk one, which I've outgrown. You shall wear it to please me, won't you, dear?" asked Belle, Annie's older sister. Meg couldn't refuse an offer so kindly made. That Thursday evening, Belle and her maid turned Meg into a fine lady. They curled her hair and put lipstick and rouge on her. They laced her into a dress that was so tight she could hardly breathe. It

was so low in the neck that modest Meg blushed at herself in the mirror. They added high-heeled silk boots, a lace handkerchief, and a fan.

At the party, Meg imagined herself acting the new part of fine lady. She did quite well, though the tight dress gave her a side-ache, and she was in constant fear that an earring would fall off and get lost or broken. She was using her fan to flirt, and was laughing at the feeble jokes of a young gentleman when she saw Laurie. She suddenly stopped laughing and looked confused. He was staring at her in surprise—and disapproval, she thought. He bowed and smiled, yet something in his honest eyes made her blush, and wish she had her old dress on.

Later, as they danced, Meg asked Laurie if he liked her dress. "No, I don't," was his blunt reply. "I don't like fuss and feathers."

Suddenly Meg saw herself as she really looked— like a doll rather than a real person. "Please don't tell them at home about my dress tonight. I'll tell them myself, and confess to Mother how silly I've been." Laurie promised not to say a word to Marmee and the girls about Meg's dress or the way she had been acting.

Meg went to sleep feeling that she hadn't enjoyed herself as much as she expected. She was glad when she finally got home two days later. As she sat there with Marmee and Jo, she said, "It does seem pleasant to be quiet and not have to use company manners all the time. Home is a nice place, though it isn't splendid." Then she told Marmee about her foolish behavior. "But it *is* nice to be admired," said Meg, looking half ashamed.

"That is perfectly natural, and quite harmless, if it does not lead one to do foolish things. Learn to value the praise that is worth having. And learn to deserve admiration by being modest as well as pretty, Meg," said Marmee. "I want each of my daughters to be beautiful, accomplished, and good. I also want them to have a happy youth, to be well and wisely married, and to lead useful, pleasant lives. To be loved and chosen by a good man is the best and sweetest thing that can happen to a woman. I hope my girls may know this beautiful experience. Remember that money is a necessary thing, but I never want you to think it is the first or only prize to strive for. I'd rather see you as poor men's wives if you are happy, than queens on thrones without self-respect and peace. Remember this, my girls: Mother is always ready to be your confidante[2], Father to be your friend. Both of us trust and hope that our daughters, whether married or single, will be the pride and comfort of our lives."

"We will, Marmee, we will!" cried Meg and Jo, with all their hearts, as they said good-night.

As spring went on, the girls had new projects to amuse them. The garden had to be put in order, and each sister had a quarter of the little plot. Each girl's section was different from the others, and reflected her personality. Meg's had roses and an orange tree. Jo's had sunflowers. Beth's had chickweed for the birds and catnip for the kittens. Amy's had honeysuckles, morning glories, and delicate ferns.

Gardening, walks, adventures on the river, and flower hunts filled the fine days. The girls also held special meetings of the "Pickwick Club." The four members of this secret society had been meeting every Saturday evening for a year. At meetings, they read aloud the newspaper they had written during the week. Each girl contributed articles, poems, stories,

---

2. **confidante** a person trusted with one's secrets

advice, and advertisements. It was a wonderful club, and the girls enjoyed it immensely.

One day, Jo stood up and suggested that they allow Laurie to join the club. At first, Meg and Amy voted no. "We don't wish for any boys. They only joke and bounce about," said Amy. "This is a ladies' club, and we wish to be private and proper."

Meg said, "I'm afraid he'll laugh at our paper."

Jo assured her sisters that Laurie would do nothing of the sort, and a second vote was unanimous. Laurie was a new member of the Pickwick Club. His first idea was to set up a post office in the hedge in the lower corner of the garden. It was an old birdhouse that was big enough to hold letters, manuscripts, books, and bundles.

The post office turned out to be great fun for the members of the Pickwick Club. All sorts of things passed through it: poetry and pickles, garden seeds and long letters, music and gingerbread, invitations and puppies. Even old Mr. Laurence amused himself by sending mysterious messages and funny telegrams. No one dreamed how many love letters that little post office would hold in the years to come!

One warm June day, Meg came home in a happy mood. "The Kings are going off to the seashore tomorrow, and I'm free. Three months of vacation—how I shall enjoy it!"

"Aunt March went to the seashore today, too. I was terribly afraid she'd ask me to go with her. If she had, I would have felt I should have had to go. But I'm so glad she didn't! It will be so nice to have some time off!"

"What will you do with your vacation?" asked Amy.

"I shall stay in bed late, and do nothing," said Meg. "I've been getting up early all winter, and have had to spend my days working for other people. Now I'm going to rest to my heart's content."

"Not me!" said Jo. "I'm going to pass the time by reading on my perch in the old apple tree."

"Let's not do any lessons, Beth, for a while. Instead, let's play and rest, like Meg and Jo," said Amy.

"Well, I will, if Mother doesn't mind. I want to learn some new songs," said Beth.

"May we, Mother?" asked Meg.

"You may try your experiment for a week, and see how you like it. I think by Saturday night you will find that all play and no work is as bad as all work and no play."

The next day, Meg did not appear till ten o'clock. She had to eat breakfast alone. The room seemed lonely and untidy, for Jo had not filled the vases, Beth had not dusted, and Amy's books lay scattered about. Nothing was neat and pleasant but "Marmee's corner," which looked as usual. Meg and Jo spent the day reading. Beth played music, glad she had no dishes to wash. Amy drew pictures under the honeysuckles.

At teatime they compared notes, and all agreed that it had been a delightful, though unusually long, day. The rest of the week went even more slowly. By Friday night, each girl said to herself that she was glad the week was nearly done. Hoping to impress the lesson more deeply, Mrs. March finished off the week by giving Hannah a holiday. When they got up on Saturday morning, there was no fire in the kitchen, no breakfast in the dining room, and no mother to be seen.

Meg ran upstairs, and soon came back again. She looked relieved, but rather bewildered. "Mother isn't sick, only very tired. She says she is going to stay quietly in her room all morning and let us do the best we can. She says it has been a hard week for her, so we mustn't grumble, but take care of ourselves."

"That's easy enough. I'm aching for something to do—that is, some new amusement," added Jo quickly.

In fact, it was a great relief to them all to have a little work to do. Meg went to the parlor, which she quickly put in order by sweeping the litter under the sofa and closing the blinds, to save the trouble of dusting. Jo, determined to have a lovely little dinner that evening, put an invitation in the post office, asking Laurie to come.

"You'd better see what we have before you think of having company," said Meg when she found out.

"Oh, there's corned beef and plenty of potatoes. I shall get some asparagus and a lobster. We'll get lettuce, and make a lobster salad. I don't know how, but the cookbook has directions. I'll have blancmange and strawberries for dessert. I'll make coffee, too, if you want to be elegant."

"Don't try too many messes, Jo, for you can't make anything but gingerbread and molasses candy. And you had better ask Mother's permission before you order anything from the grocer."

"Of course I shall," said Jo, going off in a huff.

"Get what you like. I never enjoyed housekeeping. I'm going to take a vacation today, and read, write, go visiting, and amuse myself," said Marmee.

The unusual sight of her busy mother sitting comfortably in the rocking chair reading, early in the day, made Jo feel strange. "Everything is out of sorts, somehow," she said to herself, as she piled up the dishes for washing. Later she went to the store and bought a very young lobster, some very old asparagus, and two boxes of sour strawberries.

The dinner that she took the rest of the day to prepare became a standing joke in the family. That day, Jo discovered that a good cook needs more than just energy and good will. She boiled the asparagus for an hour, and found the heads cooked off and the stalks harder than ever. The bread was burned. The lobster was so small that the little pieces of it got lost in the lettuce leaves. The potatoes were underdone, and the blancmange was lumpy.

"Well, they can eat beef, and bread and butter, if they are hungry. It's just annoying to spend the whole day working for nothing," thought Jo, as she rang the dinner bell. Poor Jo would gladly have gone under the table, as one thing after another was tasted and left. Laurie talked and laughed with all his might, to give a cheerful tone to the dinner. Jo's one strong point was the fruit, for she had sugared it well, and had a pitcher of rich cream to go with it. But even that was a disaster.

"What's wrong?" asked Jo, when Amy left the table quickly after tasting the dessert.

"Salt instead of sugar, and the cream is sour," said Meg.

Jo groaned and fell back in her chair. She remembered that she had given a last hasty powdering to the berries out of the two boxes on the kitchen table. She had forgotten to put the cream into the icebox. She turned scarlet, and was on the verge of crying. Then she met Laurie's eyes. The funny side of the dinner suddenly struck her, and she laughed till the tears ran down her cheeks. So did everyone else, and the unfortunate dinner ended happily, with bread, butter, olives, and fun.

When Marmee got home, she asked, "Are you satisfied with your experiment, girls, or do you want another week?"

"I don't!" cried Jo, and the other girls agreed.

"You think, then, it is better to have a few duties, and live a little for others? Then let me advise you to take up your little burdens again. Though they seem heavy sometimes, they are good for us. Work is wholesome. It is good for health and spirits. It gives us a sense of power and independence, which is so much better than money or fashion."

"We'll work like bees, and love it, too!" said Jo.

"Very good! It is best to have regular hours for work and play. Make each day both useful and pleasant. Prove that you understand the worth of time by using it well. Then youth will be delightful, old age will bring few regrets, and life will be a success."

"We'll remember, Mother," they said, and they did.

4 *Daydreams and Reality*

Laurie lay in his hammock[1] one warm September afternoon. He was in one of his moods, for the day had been unsatisfactory. The hot weather made him lazy. Staring up into the chestnut tree above him, he imagined himself in a boat, tossing about in the ocean, on a voyage around the world. Then the sound of voices from next door brought him ashore in a flash.

He peeked through the hedge and saw the girls setting off for the river. Meg had a cushion, Jo a book, Beth a basket, and Amy a drawing pad. "Well, that's rude—to have a picnic and not invite me," he thought. "I'll just follow them and see what's going on."

By the time Laurie found a hat, the girls were way ahead. When he caught up, he saw them sitting by the river, under a tree. Meg was sewing, Beth was sorting hemlock cones, Amy was sketching a group of ferns, and Jo was knitting as she read aloud. As soon as they saw him, they invited him to sit with them.

"We would have asked you before, but we thought you wouldn't care for such girls' games as these."

"I always like your games, but if I'm in the way, I'll go."

"You can stay, if you do something. It's against the rules to be idle here," said Meg.

"Finish this story while I fix my shoe," said Jo, handing him the book. As soon as he finished reading the story, they all started talking about their dreams for the future. Laurie told the girls that he hoped to

---

1. **hammock** a piece of rope or canvas hung from both ends and used as a bed or couch

travel the world and settle in Germany. There he would be a famous musician, and people would come from all over to hear him.

Meg's dream was to have a lovely house full of all sorts of things. She wanted to be surrounded by good food, pretty clothes, nice furniture, pleasant people, and heaps of money. She also wanted servants. "I wouldn't be idle, but do good, and make everyone love me dearly."

Jo's dream was to have a stable full of Arabian horses and rooms piled with books. "I'd write out of a magic inkstand, so that my works would be as famous as Laurie's music," declared Jo.

Beth said, "My dream is to stay at home safe with Father and Mother, and help take care of the family."

"Don't you want anything else?" asked Laurie.

"I am perfectly happy at home," said Beth.

"I have so many wishes. My favorite one is to be an artist, and go to Rome, and paint fine pictures. I want to be the best artist in the whole world," said Amy.

"If we're all alive in ten years, let's meet, and see how close we are to getting our wishes," said Jo.

"I'll be 27 by then!" exclaimed Meg.

"You and I will be 26, Laurie. Beth will be 24, and Amy 22. What a party we'll have!" said Jo.

The faint sound of a bell told them that the tea would soon be ready. They gathered their things and walked home.

"Join us again tomorrow, Laurie," said Jo. They parted at the gate.

During the month of October, Jo was very busy with her writing. She scribbled away till the last page was filled. Then she signed her name with a flourish and threw down her pen, exclaiming, "There, I've done my best!" She tied it up with a red ribbon and climbed out the back window. She took a roundabout way to the road and headed toward town.

If anyone had been watching her, he would have thought her movements very strange. Once in town, she walked to a certain busy street. She found a certain address. She went into the doorway and looked up the dirty stairs. Then she rushed back into the street and walked away as quickly as she had come. She did this several times, to the great amusement of a young gentleman watching from a nearby building. The third time, Jo pulled her hat over her eyes and walked up the stairs.

When she came back down ten minutes later, she ran into Laurie, the young gentleman who had been watching her. He had just finished his fencing[2] lesson. She could see that he was dying to know what she was doing. "It's a secret, and if I tell you, you must promise not to tell anyone," said Jo.

"I promise," said Laurie.

"I've left a story with a newspaper editor. He'll give his answer next week," whispered Jo.

"Hurrah for Miss March, the celebrated American writer!" cried Laurie. Jo's eyes sparkled. It is always pleasant to be believed in. A friend's praise is sweeter than a dozen published newspaper pieces.

For the next week or two, Jo acted so strangely that her sisters were quite puzzled. She rushed to the door every time the postman rang. One day, she bounced in and made a great show of reading something that had come in the *Post*.

"Do you have something interesting?" asked Meg.

"Nothing but a story! Won't amount to much, I guess," replied Jo.

---

2. fencing fighting with swords for sport

"What's the title?" asked Beth.

"'The Rival Painters.'" said Jo.

"That sounds good. Read it," said Meg.

So Jo took a deep breath and read the story aloud. Her sisters loved it. "Who wrote it?" asked Beth.

"Your sister," said Jo.

Dear me, how delighted they all were, to be sure! Meg wouldn't believe it till she saw the words "Miss Josephine March" actually printed in the paper. Hannah exclaimed, "Sakes alive, well, I never!" The whole family gathered around Jo and made a big fuss. These foolish, loving people made a party of every little joy.

"I didn't get paid for this first one, for the editor said they don't pay beginners. But after this, I'm not a beginner anymore. I am so happy, for in time I may be able to support myself and help the girls."

Jo's breath gave out here, and she cried a few tears. To be independent and earn the praise of those she loved were the dearest wishes of her heart. This seemed to be the first step toward that happy end.

These days of happiness were shattered one November day. The March family and Laurie were enjoying a quiet afternoon by the fire when a telegram arrived. After Mrs. March read it, she dropped back into her chair as white as if the little paper had sent a bullet to her heart. Jo picked it up and read aloud, in a frightened voice:

"Mrs. March:

Your husband is very ill. Come at once.

S. Hale.

Blank Hospital, Washington."

How still the room was as they listened breathlessly. How strangely the day darkened outside. How suddenly the whole world seemed to change. "I shall go at once, but it may be too late. Oh, children, help me to bear it!" said Marmee. "Laurie, would you send a telegram saying I will be on the next train? It leaves tomorrow morning. Would you also take a note to Aunt March's? Jo, give me that pen and paper."

Jo gave her mother some note paper, well knowing that money for the long, sad journey must be borrowed. Within moments, Laurie was off on his horse, riding as if for his life.

Beth went over to ask Mr. Laurence for a couple of bottles of old wine for Marmee to bring to Father. Mr. Brooke, who was Laurie's tutor, came over and offered his services as an escort for Mrs. March. Meg and Amy helped Marmee pack, and Jo went off to buy some hospital supplies for Marmee to take with her.

The family was just beginning to wonder where Jo was, when she came in the door. She had a very strange expression on her face. It was a mixture of fun and fear, satisfaction and regret. This puzzled the family as much as did the $25 she laid on the table before her mother. "That's my contribution toward making Father comfortable and bringing him home," said Jo.

"My dear, where did you get it?"

"I sold what was my own," said Jo, as she took off her bonnet. A general cry arose, for all her beautiful hair was cut short.

"Your hair! Oh, Jo, how could you? Your one beauty!" As everyone exclaimed, and Beth hugged the cropped head tenderly, Jo pretended she didn't care about her hair.

"Don't wail, Beth. It will be good for my vanity. I was getting too proud of my hair. It will do my brains good to have that mop taken off. My head feels nice and cool, and I'm satisfied. So please, let's have supper."

"Jo, I'm afraid you will regret it," said Marmee.

"No, I won't," said Jo.

"What made you do it?" asked Amy, who would as soon have cut off her head as her pretty hair. Jo explained how the idea had come to her as she was walking along thinking about how she could help. In a barber's window she saw tails of hair with the prices marked. One black tail, not as thick as Jo's, was $40.

At first the barber didn't want to cut Jo's hair. He said it wasn't the fashionable color. When Jo explained why she needed the money, he finally agreed to do it. The barber's wife had given Jo a long lock to keep, and Jo gave it to her mother. Mrs. March folded the wavy chestnut lock and put it in her desk.

That night, Beth could not get to sleep. Soon, she heard a sob from Jo.

"Jo, what is it? Are you crying about Father?"

"No, not now."

"What, then?"

"My—my hair!" burst out poor Jo. "I'm not sorry. I'd do it again tomorrow. It's only the vain part of me that cries in this silly way. I thought you were asleep, so I just made a little private moan for my one beauty."

5 More Problems for the Family

The next morning, Marmee left early. "Good-bye, my darlings! God bless and keep us all!" Marmee whispered, as she kissed each dear little face.

Over the next few weeks, the letters sent back and forth between Marmee and the girls kept the family close. Though Father was still dangerously ill, the presence of the best and most tender nurse of all had already done him good.

All the little duties at home were faithfully done each day. Even so, the house seemed like a clock whose pendulum[1] had gone visiting. About ten days after Mrs. March's departure, Beth said, "Meg, I wish you'd go and see the Hummels. You know Mother told us not to forget them."

"I'm too tired to go this afternoon," said Meg.

"Can't you go, Jo?" asked Beth.

"Too stormy for me with this cold."

"Why don't you go yourself?" asked Meg.

"I *have* been every day, but the baby is sick, and I don't know what to do for it. Mrs. Hummel goes away to work, and the older brother takes care of it. It gets sicker and sicker. I think you or Hannah should go."

Beth spoke earnestly, and Meg promised to go the next day. The others returned to their work. The Hummels were forgotten. About an hour later, Beth decided to go herself. As her sisters rested by the fire, she quietly put on her hood, filled her basket with food for the poor children, and went out into the chilly air.

---

1. **pendulum** in a clock, a suspended weight that swings back and forth and regulates the clock's movement

It was late when she came back. No one saw her creep upstairs. Half an hour later, Jo went upstairs, and there she found Beth, looking into the medicine chest with red eyes.

"What's the matter?" cried Jo, as Beth put out her hand as if to warn her off.

"You had scarlet fever² once, didn't you?" asked Beth.

"Years ago, when Meg had it. Why?"

"Then I'll tell you. Oh, Jo, the baby's dead!"

"What baby?"

"Mrs. Hummel's. It died in my lap before she got home," cried Beth, with a sob. "Then the doctor came and said it was scarlet fever. He told me to go home and take belladonna³ right away, or I'd get the fever."

"No, you won't!" cried Jo, hugging her close, with a frightened look.

"Don't be frightened. I don't think I'll have a bad case. I looked in Mother's book, and saw that it begins with headaches, sore throat, and strange feelings like mine. I took some belladonna, and I feel better," said Beth, trying to look well.

It turned out that Beth *did* have a bad case. Amy was sent to stay at Aunt March's, so she wouldn't come down with the fever. Meg stayed home from her job as governess, so she wouldn't infect the children. Meg and Hannah did all the housework. Jo devoted herself to Beth day and night.

Meg felt guilty when she wrote letters to Marmee without telling her of Beth's illness. She did not think

---

2. **scarlet fever** a very contagious childhood disease caused by bacteria. Symptoms include sore throat, fever, and rash.

3. **belladonna** a medicine made from the deadly nightshade plant

it was right to deceive her mother, but Hannah said not to tell her because it would only worry Mrs. March.

Beth never complained. But there came a time when during the fever fits she began to talk in a hoarse, broken voice. She played on the coverlet, as if on her beloved little piano. She tried to sing with a throat so swollen there was no music left. Then she did not know the familiar faces round her, and called them by the wrong names. She called for her mother. Then Jo grew frightened, and Meg begged Hannah to be allowed to write the truth. A letter from Washington added to their trouble. Mr. March was worse and could not think of coming home for a long while.

The first of December was a wintry day, for a bitter wind blew, snow fell fast, and the year seemed to be getting ready for its death. When the doctor came, he looked at Beth and said in a low tone, "If Mrs. March can leave her husband, she'd better be sent for." Jo immediately sent a telegram to her mother. That same day, a letter arrived saying that Mr. March was getting better. Jo read it thankfully, but the heavy weight did not seem lifted from her heart. "No one loves Beth as much as I do," she cried to Laurie. "I *can't* give her up. I can't! I can't!"

"I don't think she will die. She's so good, and we all love her so much. I don't believe God will take her away yet," said Laurie.

"The good and dear people always do die," groaned Jo, but she stopped crying, for Laurie's words were comforting. Then Laurie told Jo that he and his grandfather had already sent a telegram to Mrs. March, the day before. They had decided that Mrs. March needed to know about Beth. So, it happened that Marmee was already on the way home. The late train would be arriving at two in the morning. Laurie would pick her up.

"Laurie, you're an angel! Bless you!" said Jo.

A breath of fresh air seemed to blow through the house and something better than sunshine brightened the quiet rooms. Everything appeared to feel the hopeful change. Every time Meg and Jo met, their pale faces broke into smiles as they hugged each other, whispering, "Mother's coming, dear! Mother's coming!" Everyone rejoiced but Beth, who lay still and quiet. Every now and then she muttered, "Water!" with lips so parched they could hardly shape the word.

Night came at last. The doctor had been in to say that some change, for better or worse, would probably take place about midnight. The girls never forgot that night, for no sleep came to them as they kept their watch.

"I wish I had no heart, it aches so," sighed Meg.

"If life is often as hard as this, I don't see how we ever shall get through it," added Jo.

When the clock struck midnight, they thought they saw a change pass over Beth's face. An hour went by, and nothing happened except for Laurie's quiet departure for the train station. Another hour—still no one came. Anxious fears of delay in the storm, an accident, or worst of all, a great grief in Washington, haunted the girls.

At two o'clock, Jo looked at Beth and thought a great change had taken place. The fever flush and the look of pain were gone. The beloved little face looked so peaceful that Jo felt no desire to weep, even though she thought her sister had died. She kissed Beth's forehead and softly whispered, "Good-bye, my Beth, good-bye!"

Suddenly Hannah woke up, hurried to the bed, and

looked at Beth. She exclaimed, "The fever's turned. She's sleeping comfortably and breathing easily. Praise be given! Oh, my goodness me!"

Just then, the doctor came. "Yes, my dears, I think the little girl will pull through this time."

"If Mother would only come now!" said Jo, as the dark winter night came to an end. Never had the sun risen so beautifully. Never had the world seemed so lovely as it did to Meg and Jo that morning. "Listen!" cried Jo, jumping to her feet.

Yes, there was a sound of bells at the door below and a cry from Hannah. Then there was Laurie's voice saying, in a joyful whisper, "Girls, she's come, she's come!"

I don't think I have any words to tell about the meeting of the mother and daughters. Such hours are beautiful to live, but very hard to describe. I will leave it to the imagination of my readers. When Beth woke from her sleep, the first thing she saw was her mother's face. Too weak to wonder at anything, she only smiled. Then she slept again.

Marmee would not leave Beth's side. She rested in the big chair, waking often to touch and brood over her child, like a miser over some recovered treasure.

While all these things were happening at home, Amy was having hard times at Aunt March's. She had to wash the cups every morning, and polish the old-fashioned spoons, the fat silver teapot, and the glasses till they shone. Then she had to dust the room. What a trying job that was! Not a speck escaped Aunt March's eye, and all the furniture had claw legs and much carving. It was never dusted well enough to please Aunt March. Laurie came to visit every day, which helped pass about an hour each afternoon. Amy looked forward to hearing some good news about Beth, for she longed to return home to her family's loving arms.

One afternoon, Marmee and Jo had a long talk. Marmee told Jo that John was in love with Meg.

"Who?" asked Jo, staring at her mother.

"Mr. Brooke, Laurie's tutor. I call him 'John' now. We got to know him very well at the hospital, when he was helping with your father. He was perfectly open and honorable about Meg. He told us he loved her, but would earn a comfortable home before he asked her to marry him. He only asked for our permission to love her and work for her. He is a truly excellent young man. Jo, I don't wish you to say anything to Meg yet. When John comes back, and I see them together, I can judge her feelings toward him better. If she and John love each other, they can wait until she is 20 before they marry."

"I knew there was mischief brewing," Jo said. "I just wish I could marry Meg and keep her safe in the family."

"It is natural that you should all go to your own homes," Marmee said. "But I am sorry this happened so soon. My pretty, tender-hearted girl! I hope things go happily with her."

"Wouldn't you rather have her marry a rich man?" asked Jo.

"Money is a good and useful thing, Jo, and I hope my girls will always have enough. I am content to see Meg begin humbly, for she will be rich in the possession of a good man's heart, and that is better than a fortune."

6 *Happy Surprises*

Jo was not very good at keeping secrets, and she was really afraid Laurie would get this one out of her. She was quite right, for the mischief-loving lad no sooner suspected a mystery than he set himself to find it out. He begged, bribed, and scolded until he finally satisfied himself that it involved Meg and Mr. Brooke, even though Jo did not actually tell him anything. Feeling hurt that he had not been taken into his tutor's confidence, he decided to do something to get back at him.

A day later, a change seemed to come over Meg. She blushed a lot, was very quiet, and had a timid, troubled look on her face.

"Here's a note to you, Meg, all sealed up. How odd! Laurie never seals mine," said Jo, a few days later, handing out the contents of the little post office. A moment later, Mrs. March and Jo were surprised to hear a startled sound from Meg. They saw her staring at the note with a frightened face.

"My child, what is it?" cried her mother.

"It's all a mistake—he didn't send it. Oh, Jo, how could you do it?" Meg hid her face in her hands, crying as if her heart were broken.

"Me! I've done nothing!" cried Jo, bewildered.

Meg's eyes were angry as she pulled a different, crumpled note from her pocket, and threw it at Jo. "You wrote this, and Laurie helped you. How could you be so mean?" Jo and her mother read the note, which was written in a strange handwriting.

"My dearest Meg,
I can no longer keep my love for you a secret. I dare
not tell your parents yet, but I think they would
approve if they knew that we adored one another.
Please send one word of hope to me through Laurie.
Your devoted John."

Meg told them she had received the note a few days
before. "I meant to tell you, Marmee. Then I remembered how you liked Mr. Brooke, so I thought you
wouldn't mind if I kept my little secret for a few days.
Now I've really paid for my silliness, and I can never
look him in the face again."

"What did you say to him?" asked Mrs. March.

"I only said I was too young to do anything about it
yet. I told him I didn't wish to keep secrets from my
parents, and he must speak to Father. I said I was
grateful for his kindness, and would be his friend, but
nothing more, for a long while."

"What did he say to that?" asked Jo.

"He wrote the letter that I received today. He said
he had never sent a love letter at all, and was sorry
that Jo would take such liberties with our names."

Jo tramped about the room calling Laurie names.
All of a sudden she stopped, picked up the two notes,
and looked at them closely. Then she said, "I don't
believe Mr. Brooke ever saw either of these letters.
Laurie wrote them both, that little villain!"

Marmee sent Jo over to get Laurie, and as soon as
he saw Mrs. March's face, he knew why he had been
sent for. For the next half hour, Mrs. March spoke to
Laurie alone in the parlor. Then Meg and Jo were
called in. Laurie apologized and assured Meg that
John Brooke knew nothing about either letter. Meg
accepted Laurie's apology, but Jo did not. As soon as he

left, Jo wished she had been more forgiving. Later, she went over to the big house to make her own apologies to Laurie.

Laurie was in a very bad mood, for he had just had a big scene with his grandfather. When Mr. Laurence had asked Laurie why Mrs. March had sent for him, Laurie had refused to answer. He said to Jo, "I promised your mother I would not tell why she wanted me. When I told him that I could say nothing, he should have just dropped it. He should apologize for the way he acted. Since he won't, I think I'll just take a trip somewhere. Maybe I'll go and visit Mr. Brooke in Washington. When Grandpa misses me, he'll apologize."

"If I get your grandpa to apologize, will you give up running away?" asked Jo.

"Yes, but you won't be able to do it," said Laurie.

Jo went to the library to talk to Mr. Laurence. It turned out that he thought Laurie had done something ungrateful or rude. "If he has, after all your kindness to him, I'll thrash him with my own hands."

Jo explained that she could not tell him what had happened. "Laurie has confessed, asked pardon, and been punished quite enough. We don't keep silence to protect him, but someone else. It will make more trouble if you interfere," said Jo.

Finally, Jo was able to get Mr. Laurence to write an apology. "A formal apology will make him see how foolish he is. Try it. He likes fun, and this way is better than talking. I'll carry it up to him," she said. Mr. Laurence wrote a note of apology to his grandson, and Jo delivered it, bringing peace to the Laurence household.

The next few weeks were like sunshine after a storm. Mr. March and Beth were both improving rapidly, and Mr. March began to talk of returning early in the new year. Beth was soon able to lie on the sofa in the study all day, but she was still very weak.

As Christmas approached, Jo and Laurie worked on a secret plan to surprise the family. On Christmas Eve, they worked during the night and created a stately snow maiden in the garden. She was holding a basket of fruit and flowers in one hand and a big roll of new music in the other. There was a new blanket around her chilly shoulders and a pink paper streamer coming from her lips. On the streamer was a long poem to Beth, written by Jo. How Beth laughed when she saw it. How Laurie ran up and down to bring in the gifts! What silly speeches Jo made as she presented them!

"I'm so full of happiness that, if Father was only here, I couldn't hold one drop more," said Beth.

"So am I," said Jo. Meg, Amy, and Marmee agreed. Half an hour after everyone had said they were so happy they could only hold one drop more, the drop appeared. Laurie opened the parlor door, and popped his head in very quietly.

"Here's another Christmas present for the March family," he said. Before the words were out of his mouth, Father appeared, leaning on the arm of John Brooke. Of course there was a general stampede, and Mr. March became invisible in the embrace of many loving arms. Even Beth was able to get up to hug him, for joy put strength into her feeble limbs. A few minutes later, John suddenly remembered that Mr. March needed rest. Taking Laurie, he left. Then the two invalids were ordered to rest, which they did, by both sitting in one big chair and talking.

There never *was* such a Christmas dinner as they had that day. The fat turkey was a sight to behold, when Hannah served it up, stuffed, browned, and decorated. Mr. Laurence and his grandson dined with them, and so did Mr. Brooke. A sleigh ride had been planned, but the girls would not leave their father. The happy family sat around the fire and counted their blessings for the rest of the evening.

The next day, Jo told Meg, "Laurie's mischief has changed you. I see it, and so does Mother. You are not like your old self a bit, and you seem ever so far away from me. I do wish it was all settled," said Jo.

"*I* can't say anything till he speaks, and he won't because Father said I was too young," said Meg.

"If he did speak, you would cry or blush, instead of giving a good, firm 'No.'"

"I'm not as silly and weak as you think. I know just what I will say, for I've planned it all," said Meg.

"Would you mind telling me what you'd say?"

"Not at all. I would say, calmly and firmly, 'Thank you, Mr. Brooke, you are very kind, but I agree with Father that I am too young to be engaged. Please say no more, but let us be friends as we were.'"

"I don't believe you'll ever say it. I know he won't be satisfied if you do. If he acts like the rejected lovers in books, you'll give in rather than hurt his feelings."

"No, I won't. I shall tell him I've made up my mind, and shall walk out of the room with dignity." Meg rose as she spoke. She was going to rehearse the dignified exit when Mr. Brooke came to the door. Jo quickly excused herself to give Meg a chance to make her speech. As soon as Jo left, Mr. Brooke took Meg's hand and looked at her with so much love in his brown eyes that her heart began to flutter.

"I won't trouble you. I only want to know if you care for me a little, Meg. I love you so much, dear," said Mr. Brooke tenderly. Meg forgot every word of her speech as her heart beat fast, but then she remembered what she had planned to say. She told John that she wasn't ready to be engaged at all. What might have happened next I cannot say, if Aunt March had not come in at that interesting moment.

She had come over to see her nephew, and she overheard part of the conversation between Meg and Mr. Brooke. After Mr. Brooke had left the room, Aunt March told Meg, "If you marry that poor tutor, not one penny of my money will go to you. Remember that, and be sensible."

Now, as soon as Aunt March ordered Meg *not* to love John, Meg made up her mind that she would. "I shall marry whom I please, Aunt March, and you can leave your money to anyone you like," she said.

"So, you intend to marry a man without money, position, or business, and go on working harder than you do now, when you could do so much better?"

"I couldn't do better if I waited half my life! John is good and wise. He has heaps of talent, he's willing to work, and he's sure to succeed. Everyone likes and respects him, and I'm proud to think he cares for me, though I'm so poor and young and silly," said Meg.

After Aunt March had left, John came in. "I couldn't help hearing, Meg. Thank you for defending me. And I need not go away? I may stay and be happy?"

"Yes, John," Meg whispered. Within minutes, they were engaged. They would have to wait three years. By then, Meg would be 20, and John would have earned enough for them to start a home.

7 Big Changes

Three years passed, bringing a few changes to the quiet family. The war ended, and Mr. March was safely at home. He was busy with his books and with the small parish where he was now the minister.

John Brooke had been to war and come back after having been wounded. He received no stars or bars, but he deserved them. He cheerfully risked all he had, and life and love are very precious when both are in full bloom. He was now working as a bookkeeper, earning a salary and saving for his marriage to Meg.

Meg's friend Sallie had married Ned Moffat. Meg couldn't help contrasting their fine home with her own. Sometimes she secretly wished she could have the same. But envy vanished when she thought of all the love John had put into the little home awaiting her. When she talked with John about their future, she forgot Sallie's wealth and felt herself the richest, happiest girl in the world.

Jo never went back to Aunt March's, for the old lady had taken a liking to Amy. She had bribed her with the offer of drawing lessons. So, Amy devoted her mornings to duty and her afternoons to pleasure. Jo devoted herself to literature and Beth, whose health still remained delicate. She was not an invalid, but she was not the rosy, healthy creature she had been.

Laurie had gone to college to please his grandfather. He was trying to get through it as easily as possible. He often brought friends home from school, and Amy quickly became a favorite among them. Meg was too absorbed with John to pay any attention, and Beth was too shy to do anything more than peep at them. They all liked Jo, but never fell in love with her. Most of them sighed at Amy's shrine. And speaking of sentiment brings us very naturally to the "Dovecote."[1]

This was the name of the little brown house that John had prepared for Meg's first home. It was a tiny house with a little garden and a lawn about as big as a pocket handkerchief. Inside, it was charming.

To be sure, the hall was very narrow and the dining room so small that six people were a tight fit. But good sense and good taste had helped choose the furniture. There were no marble-topped tables, long mirrors, or lace curtains in the little parlor. Simple furniture, plenty of books, a fine picture, and flowers in the bay window made the house quite cozy.

No storeroom was ever better provided with good wishes, merry words, and happy hopes than Meg's. There, Jo and Marmee had put away Meg's few boxes, barrels, and bundles. I am certain that the new kitchen never could have looked so cozy and neat if Hannah had not arranged every pot and pan a dozen times over. I doubt if any young wife ever began life with so many cleaning cloths. Beth had made enough of them to last for 25 years.

The day of the wedding finally arrived. The June roses over the porch were awake bright and early on that morning. Meg looked like a rose herself. All that was best and sweetest in heart and soul seemed to bloom in her face that day. She wore neither silk nor lace. "I don't want to look strange or fixed up today," she said. "I don't want a fashionable wedding. I only want to be surrounded by those I love."

She had made her wedding gown herself, sewing

---

1. **dovecote**   a small house for tame pigeons

into it the tender hopes of a girlish heart. Her sisters braided up her pretty hair. The only ornaments she wore were the lilies of the valley which "her John" liked best of all the flowers that grew.

"Please hug and kiss me, everyone. Don't mind my dress. I want a great many wrinkles of this sort put into it today," said Meg, opening her arms to her sisters. They hugged her tightly, feeling that her new love had not changed the old. All three of Meg's sisters looked just what they were—fresh-faced, happy-hearted girls, pausing a moment in their busy lives to read the sweetest chapter in the romance of womanhood.

It was a simple ceremony, followed by a simple but festive reception. They ate in the dining room and danced in the garden outside. Then the guests said their good-byes. The only bridal journey Meg had was the quiet walk with John from the old home to the new. Before she left, Meg said, "Don't feel that I am separated from you, Marmee dear, or that I love you any less for loving John so much. I shall come every day, Father, and expect to keep my old place in all your hearts, though I am married. Thank you for my happy wedding day. Good-bye, good-bye!"

They stood watching her, with faces full of love and hope and tender pride, as she walked away, leaning on her husband's arm. And so Meg's married life began.

Amy spent the next few months trying every branch of art with youthful boldness. She tried pen-and-ink drawings, wood-burning, and oil painting. She tried charcoal portraits, crayon sketches, clay, and plaster. Her efforts with plaster, however, were brought to a quick end by an accident. One day, she decided to cast her own pretty foot, and soon the family was alarmed by her screams. Running to the rescue, they found the young artist hopping wildly about the shed. Her foot was held fast in a panful of plaster that had hardened too quickly. With much difficulty and some danger, she was dug out. Jo was so overcome with laughter that her knife went too far. It cut poor Amy's foot, leaving a lasting scar of one artistic attempt.

After this, Amy left the plaster alone. Soon her mania for sketching from nature brought her to rivers, fields, and woods. She caught endless colds sitting on damp grass to do her sketches. She got a sunburn floating on the river in the midsummer sun, studying light and shade.

Meanwhile, she was learning, doing, and enjoying other things, too. She had decided to be an attractive and accomplished woman, even if she never became a great artist. Here she did better, for she pleased without effort and made friends everywhere. Everyone liked her. One of her weaknesses was a desire to move in "our best society," without being sure what the best really was. Money, position, and manners were important to her.

One day she asked Marmee to have a party for the girls in her drawing class. It was to be a luncheon party, and it would include a row on the river. Amy wanted only the finest of foods. She said she would pay for it herself.

Mrs. March knew that experience was an excellent teacher. She told Amy to go ahead with her plans.

Jo said, "Why would you spend your money, worry your family, and turn the house upside down for a group of girls who don't even care about you?"

"They do care for me, and I for them. You don't care to make people like you, to go into good society, and cultivate your manners and tastes. I do, and I mean to make the most of every chance that comes," said Amy.

The invitations were sent and nearly all accepted.

The following Monday was set for the grand event. Amy decorated the house with flowers and art. The lunch looked charming. Then it began to rain.

The young ladies were to come the next day in case of foul weather. Amy got up at dawn again. She decorated the house and prepared the food.

Imagine Amy's disappointment when only one guest showed up. Miss Eliott was her name, and she found the family charming. They enjoyed the delicious lunch, visited the studio and the garden, and discussed art with enthusiasm.

Finally, the afternoon came to an end, and Miss Eliott went home. "Bundle everything into a basket, and send it to the Hummels," said Amy as soon as Miss Eliott was gone.

"I'm very sorry you were disappointed, dear," said Mrs. March, in a tone full of motherly regret.

"It's not my fault that the party failed. I comfort myself with that," said Amy. "I thank you all for helping me. I'll thank you still more if you say nothing about this for a month, at least."

During that month, and the next, Jo spent hours working on her novel with all her heart and soul. She felt that she could find no peace until it was finished. She did not think herself a genius by any means, but whenever the writing fit came on, she gave herself up to it. Then she led a blissful life, safe and happy in an imaginary world, full of friends almost as real to her as any in the flesh. She could barely sleep or eat during these writing periods that lasted a week or two. Then she would emerge, hungry, sleepy, or cross.

She was just recovering from one of these writing fits when she was invited to a lecture. While she was there, she saw a young man reading a newspaper story about love, mystery, and murder. They started talking about the author, and the young man mentioned that she had written a lot of stories, and he had read them all. "She knows just what folks like, and gets paid well for writing it," he told her.

Jo decided to write such a story. Secretly, she entered a contest and won a $100 prize. Of course, there was a big celebration at home at this news, even though her father said, "You can write better than this, Jo. Aim at the highest, and never mind the money."

Still, the money was useful, and with it Jo sent Marmee and Beth to the seashore for a month. Over the next year, she won several more of those delightful checks. "The Duke's Daughter" paid the butcher's bill. "A Phantom Hand" put down a new carpet. And the "Curse of the Coventrys" bought groceries and gowns.

Finally, she got back to her novel and was able to finish it. One publisher said he would publish it if she cut it down one third. Just to get it printed, she agreed. She was paid $300 for the novel, which came in handy. But Jo was confused by the mixed reviews it got.

One critic called it "an exquisite book, full of truth, beauty, and earnestness." Another said it was bad and full of "unnatural characters." Jo didn't know what to think. She decided that she had cut out all the best parts. "Next time," she told her mother, "I'll print the whole book or none of it, for I do hate to be so misjudged."

8 Punishments and Rewards

Meg began her married life determined to be a model housekeeper. It was her greatest hope that John should find home a paradise. He should always see a smiling face. He should eat like a king every day. He should never know the loss of a button. She brought so much love, energy, and cheerfulness to the work that she could not but succeed. Her paradise was not perfect, however.

Sometimes she was too tired even to smile. John did not like fancy food and ungratefully asked for plain dishes. As for buttons, she soon began to wonder where they went, shaking her head over the carelessness of men. She threatened to make him sew them on himself.

One day, she decided to make currant jelly. It looked easy enough when she had watched Hannah do it. John bought 48 little pots and half a barrel of sugar. Meg spent the whole day boiling, straining, and fussing over her jelly. She did her best, but the dreaded stuff would not jell. Finally, she sat down in her topsy-turvy kitchen, lifted up her voice, and wept.

As if she didn't have enough troubles, John decided to bring a friend home for dinner that day. He didn't think to check with Meg first. She had often said he should feel free to bring a friend home whenever he liked. When John found that no dinner was ready and that Meg refused to even meet the friend, they had their first disagreement. Meg stayed upstairs while John and his friend Mr. Scott found whatever they could in the kitchen. Later that evening, after Mr.

Scott left, Meg and John spent several hours ignoring each other. They finally made up, and all was well again.

In the autumn, Meg and Sallie Moffat renewed their friendship. One day, when they were out shopping, Meg gave in to a terrible temptation. She spent $50 on 25 yards of lovely violet silk for a new party dress. Sallie had urged her to do it, and had even offered to lend her the money, but Meg had used money from the household fund. When John found out about it, he said, "Twenty-five yards of silk seems a good deal to cover one small woman."

Meg said, "I know you are angry, John, but I can't help it. I don't mean to waste your money, but I can't resist when I see Sallie buying all she wants, and pitying me because I don't. I try to be contented, but it is hard. I'm tired of being poor."

These words wounded John deeply, for he had denied himself many pleasures for Meg's sake. She could have bitten her tongue the minute she said it. John said, "I was afraid of this. I do my best, Meg." Meg felt terrible. She had promised to love him for better or worse, and then she had complained about his poverty, after spending his money foolishly. She felt even worse when she found out that he canceled his order for a new coat later that week. When she asked him why, he said, "I can't afford it, my dear."

Next day she put her pride in her pocket, went to Sallie, told the truth, and asked her to buy the silk as a favor. Sallie did so, and had the good sense not to make Meg a present of it immediately afterward.

That very day, Meg bought the new coat for John. When he got home, she put it on and asked him how he liked her new silk gown. One can imagine what answer he made, how he received his present, and how happy the young couple was after that. So the year rolled around. At midsummer there came to Meg a new experience—the deepest and tenderest of a woman's life.

When Laurie came to see Meg and John's baby, Jo made him sit down and close his eyes. Then she put the little bundle in his arms. When Laurie opened his eyes, he found that he was holding not one baby, but two! The twins were named Margaret and John Laurence, and nicknamed Daisy and Demi.

One day in the middle of July, shortly after the birth of the twins, Amy made Jo keep her promise to go visiting one afternoon. "I can hardly believe I told you I'd make six calls in one day, when a single one upsets me for a week," said Jo.

"Well, you did. The bargain was that I would finish the drawing of Beth for you, and you would go with me to return our neighbors' visits."

"I'll go if I must, and I'll do my best to be sociable. Let's get it over with," said Jo.

"You're an angel," said Amy. "Now put on your best things, and I'll tell you how to behave at each place. I want people to like you. They would, if you'd only try to be more agreeable." After Amy had made sure that Jo was dressed properly, they set out for their first call.

"Now, Jo dear, the Chesters are very elegant people, so I want you to behave. Don't do anything odd, will you? Just be calm, cool, and quiet. That's safe and ladylike, and you can easily do it for 15 minutes."

Naughty Jo took Amy at her word. During the first call, she sat there, calm as a summer sea, cool as a snowbank, and silent as a statue. Every question about her "charming novel," parties, picnics, the opera, and fashion was answered by a smile, a bow, and a "Yes" or "No." In vain Amy signaled the word "Talk," and tried to draw Jo out. Nothing worked.

On the way to their second visit, Amy said, "Try to be sociable at the Lambs', gossip as the other girls do, be interested in dress and whatever nonsense comes up. They move in the best society and are valuable people for us to know."

"I'll be agreeable. I'll gossip and giggle, and have raptures over any trifle you like. I rather enjoy this, and now I'll imitate what is called 'a charming girl.' I can do it, for I have May Chester as a model, and I'll improve upon her," said Jo. For the first half hour of their visit, Jo gushed as well as any silly girl. Amy could do nothing to stop her. No matter what subject was brought up, Jo thought it was "perfectly splendid," and she laughed at every joke.

Then the elder Miss Lamb said, "We read a story of yours the other day, and enjoyed it very much."

Any mention of her stories always had a bad effect on Jo. She answered, "Sorry you could find nothing better to read. I write that rubbish because it sells, and ordinary people like it."

Since Miss Lamb had "enjoyed" the story, this speech was not exactly complimentary. The minute she said it, Jo saw her mistake. Afraid to make matters worse, she suddenly made a move to leave. She did it so abruptly that three people were left with half-finished sentences in their mouths.

"Amy, we *must* go. *Good-bye*, dear. Do come and see us. We are *pining* for a visit," she said. She was imitating May Chester's gushing style so well that Amy got out of the room as quickly as possible. She had a strong desire to laugh and cry at the same time.

"What is wrong with you, Jo?" she asked. "You never will learn how to act properly."

"I thought I did a good job! How shall I behave

here?" asked Jo, as they got to the third mansion.

"Just as you please. I wash my hands of you."

"Then I'll enjoy myself. The boys are at home, and we'll have a comfortable time," said Jo. By the time Amy was ready to leave, she found Jo sitting on the grass. A group of boys was around her, and a dirty-footed dog lying on her best skirt.

At the fourth and fifth houses, Amy and Jo just left their cards,[1] for nobody was home. The sixth visit was to Aunt March. When they got there, they found that Aunt Carrol was already visiting. They dropped their conversation as soon as the girls came in. It was clear that they had been talking about their nieces.

After the girls had been welcomed, and some small talk was made, the subject of charity came up. Amy had volunteered some of her time at an art fair. The profits would be going to a good cause. Amy said she was glad to help.

"Good for you, dear," said Aunt March. "I think you'll find that it's always a pleasure to help people who appreciate our efforts. Some do not, and that is upsetting."

If Jo had only known what a great happiness was wavering in the balance for one of them, she would have held her tongue. But she made a big mistake right then, one that she would later regret. "I don't like favors. They burden me and make me feel like a slave," she said. "I'd rather do everything for myself, and be perfectly independent."

Aunt Carrol looked at Aunt March. "I told you so," said Aunt March, nodding to Aunt Carrol.

"Do you speak French, dear?" asked Aunt Carrol,

---

1. **cards** calling cards, sometimes called visiting cards, with a person's name on them, presented when visiting someone

laying her hand on Amy's.

"Pretty well," said Amy.

"How about you?" asked Aunt Carrol of Jo.

"Don't know a word. I can't bear French. It's such a slippery, silly sort of language," Jo answered.

Another look passed between the ladies.

It was a week or so before Jo found out what a big mistake she had made. A letter came from Aunt Carrol, inviting Amy to go with her on a long trip to Europe. When Jo objected, saying she was older and should be the one to go, Marmee read from Aunt Carrol's letter. "I planned at first to ask Jo. But she said that 'favors burden her' and she 'can't bear French,' so I think that Amy would get more out of the experience."

Jo tried to hide her disappointment. She didn't want to sadden Amy's pleasure by her own regrets. Soon, Amy sailed away to find the old world, which is always new and beautiful to young eyes.

The letters that arrived at the March house over the next few months described Amy's impressions of London, Paris, and Heidelberg. Amy also told the family about her flirtation with Fred Vaughn, one of Laurie's English friends. "If Fred asks me to marry him, I shall accept him, though I'm not madly in love. I like him, and we get on comfortably together. He is handsome, young, and very rich—ever so much richer than the Laurences. One of us *must* marry well. Meg didn't, Jo won't, Beth can't yet, so I shall, and make everything cozy all around."

9 *Laurie's Great Disappointment*

"Jo, I'm worried about Beth," said Marmee.

"Why, Marmee? She seems better since the babies came."

"It's not her health that worries me now. It's her spirits. I'm sure there is something on her mind, and I want you to find out what it is."

"What makes you think so, Marmee?"

"She sits alone a good deal, and she doesn't talk to her father as much as she used to. When she sings, her songs are always sad ones. Now and then, I see a look in her face that I don't understand."

"I think she's growing up. Beth's now 18, but we don't realize it. We treat her like a child, forgetting she's a woman," said Jo. "I'll talk to her and try to find out what's on her mind, if it will make you feel better."

For the next few days, Jo kept a close watch on Beth. She noticed that Beth was unhappy, except when she saw Laurie. "How strong and well and happy that dear boy looks," said Beth one afternoon, as Laurie waved from outside.

"Mercy on me, Beth loves Laurie!" Jo decided. "If he doesn't love her back, how dreadful it would be. He must! I'll make him!" Then she thought about Laurie, and how he always flirted with Amy and joked with Jo. But he had always treated Beth with special kindness and gentleness. But then, everybody treated Beth that way, so no one imagined that Laurie cared more for her than the others. Indeed, the general feeling had been that Laurie was sweet on Jo. Sometimes his teasing and flirting seemed to prove it.

One night, just as Jo was dropping off to sleep, she heard a sob that made her fly to Beth's bedside.

"What is it, dear?" she asked. "Is it the old pain?"

"No, it's a new one, but I can bear it," answered Beth. Her hand went to her heart, as if the pain were there. "I'll be better soon."

Even though Jo thought she knew the reason for Beth's new pain, she said, "Is anything wrong, dear?"

"Yes, but I can't tell you yet," said Beth.

Finally Beth fell asleep, but Jo stayed awake for a long time, thinking. The next day, Jo went to Marmee with a new plan.

"I want something new. I feel restless, and I want to see, do, and learn more. I'd like to go to New York. I can live in your friend Mrs. Kirke's boardinghouse and teach her children and sew. While I'm there, I shall see and hear new things and get new ideas. I'll bring home all kinds of new material to write about."

"I see, dear. Are these your only reasons for wanting to go to New York?"

"No, Marmee. Part of the reason is that I'm afraid Laurie is getting too fond of me."

"Then you don't care for him in the way it is clear he cares for you?" asked Mrs. March.

"Mercy, no! I love the dear boy, as I always have— like a brother. But as for anything more, it's out of the question."

Arrangements were made for Jo to live in New York at Mrs. Kirke's boardinghouse. The teaching would pay enough so Jo would be independent. During her leisure time, she could write. Jo was looking forward to the change, for the home nest was growing too narrow for her adventurous spirit.

Before she left, she said to Beth, "I am leaving one thing to your special care."

"You mean your papers?" asked Beth.

"No, I mean Laurie. Be good to him, won't you?"

"Of course I will, but I can't fill your place. He'll miss you sadly."

When Laurie said good-bye, he whispered to Jo, "It won't do a bit of good. My eye is on you. So mind what you do, or I'll come and bring you home."

As soon as Jo settled in at Mrs. Kirke's, she started writing a journal. Each week she mailed the journal home to Marmee and Beth, to tell them about her activities.

In the first week's installment, she told them all about her room. It had a stove, a nice table by a sunny window, and a fine view that included a church tower. She told them how she enjoyed writing at that pleasant table, and how much she liked teaching Mrs. Kirke's two little girls. She also told them about an interesting man who lived at the boardinghouse. His name was Professor Bhaer, a kind and well-learned man from Berlin. He gave lessons to support himself and his two little orphaned nephews, who had been left in his care.

In her second letter, Jo told Marmee and Beth more about Professor Bhaer. He was "a regular German— rather stout, with brown hair tumbled all over his head, a bushy beard, good nose, the kindest eyes I ever saw, and a splendid voice." Jo went on to describe the way Professor Bhaer treated his little students. He was the picture of patience and affection, and his students seemed to love him.

In each journal entry that Jo sent home, she told more about the kindly Professor Bhaer. She described how she had been on her way out for a walk, when by accident she bumped her umbrella against his door. The door flew open, and there stood Professor Bhaer with a big blue sock in one hand and a darning needle in the other. "It was a little pathetic to think of the poor man having to mend his own clothes," she wrote.

In another entry, Jo described to Marmee and Beth how she had come upon Professor Bhaer one Saturday, playing with the children who lived in the boardinghouse. He was the "effalunt," and such an elephant! "A more glorious frolic I never saw," Jo wrote home. "They played tag and soldiers, and piled on the sofa next to the professor, who told charming fairy stories."

Over the next few months, Jo's letters were full of news about her life in the boardinghouse. She had begun to take lessons in German from the professor, in exchange for doing some of his mending.

Jo spent Christmas that year in New York, and received a big package of gifts from home. She wrote to Marmee and Beth about how Mr. Bhaer had given everyone in the boardinghouse a gift. "Poor as he is, he didn't forget a servant or a child in the house, and not a soul here forgot him, either. I was so glad of that," she said. Mr. Bhaer gave Jo a copy of Shakespeare's plays and sonnets. She gave him a vase for the flowers he always liked to keep on his desk.

As the New Year arrived, Jo thought she was doing very well. She wrote home, "I feel as if I am getting on a little in spite of my many failures. I'm cheerful all the time now, work with a will, and take more interest in other people than I used to, which is good."

In spite of everything going on around her, Jo found time to write stories. She could see that money meant power. She made up her mind to have some money, not for herself alone, but for those whom she loved. She wanted to give Beth everything she wanted, from strawberries in winter to an organ in her bedroom.

The prize-story experience had seemed to show her

how to get the money she wanted, but reaction to the novel had confused her. Enough time had passed, however, since the negative criticism had appeared in print. Jo was finally ready to get back to work.

She took to writing sensation stories, for in those days even all-perfect America read rubbish. Her first story was accepted, on the condition that she cut out certain parts to "make it just the right length," in the editor's words. As she looked at the marked pages of her manuscript, she felt as though something very dear had been taken away. All the moral reflections had been crossed out.

"But, sir, I thought every story should have some sort of a moral, so I took care to have a few of my sinners repent," she said.

"People want to be amused, not preached at, you know," said the editor. "We pay from $25 to $30 for stories like this. We'll pay when it's printed."

Over the next few months, Jo continued to turn out stories. Her thin purse grew much fatter, and her plans to take Beth to the mountains next summer seemed more likely to come true. Eager to find material for stories, and determined to make them original, she searched newspapers for accidents and crimes. She read books on poisons. She studied faces in the street. She tried to imagine folly, sin, and misery so she could write about them.

In one of their conversations, Mr. Bhaer advised her to instead study simple, true, and lovely characters. That, he said, was good training for a writer. Jo took him at his word, and began to study him.

Why everybody liked him was what puzzled Jo, at first. He was neither rich nor great, young nor handsome. He was not fascinating or brilliant. Yet, people seemed to gather about him as naturally as they did around a warm hearth. He was poor, yet always seemed to be giving something away. As Jo watched him, trying to discover his charm, she decided it was his goodness that drew people to him.

One day, Jo and Mr. Bhaer began to talk about the sensational stories in the newspapers. "I would rather give my boys gunpowder to play with than such trash," he said.

"If there is a demand for it, I don't see any harm in supplying it. Many very respectable people make an honest living out of these sensational stories," Jo said.

"There is a demand for whiskey, but I think you and I do not care to sell it," said Mr. Bhaer.

That evening, when she went up to her room, Jo reread every one of her stories. Their faults glared at her. "They *are* trash," she thought. "I've written them for money, and I can't help being ashamed of them. What would I do if someone at home saw them, or if Mr. Bhaer read them?"

With that, she stuffed the whole bundle into her stove. In two minutes, she had burned three months' worth of work. She wrote no more sensational stories after that, but she didn't really know what else to write.

Before she knew it, it was June, and the school year had ended. It was time to return home. Everyone seemed sorry when that time came, especially Mr. Bhaer. He had fallen in love with Jo. "It is not time for me. I must not hope for it now," he said to himself.

As for Jo, she thought, "Well, the winter's gone, and I've written no books and earned no fortune. But I've made a friend worth having, and I'll try to keep him all my life."

Jo was happy to get home. Laurie graduated with honors from college, and Jo was home in time to go to the ceremony. She could tell just by looking at him that Laurie was getting ready to propose to her. Then she thought that she must have misread his face. Surely he would not propose when she had given every clue about what her answer would be. But her first instincts were correct. Laurie went on with the proposal even after she said, "Laurie, please don't."

"I will, and you *must* hear me. It's no use, Jo. We've got to have it out, and the sooner the better for both of us. I've loved you ever since I've known you. I couldn't help it. I've tried to show it, but you wouldn't let me. Now I'm going to make you hear, and give me an answer. I *can't* go on like this any longer."

"I am so fond of you, Laurie," said Jo. "I don't see why I can't love you as you want me to. I've tried, but I can't. It would be a lie to say I do when I don't."

"Really, truly, Jo?" He stopped short, caught both her hands in his, and looked at her with an expression that she did not soon forget.

"Really, truly, dear." They were in the grove, right by the fence. As Jo said this, Laurie dropped her hands and turned as if to go. But then, he just laid his head down on a mossy fence post, and stood so still that Jo was frightened.

"Oh, Laurie, I'm sorry, so desperately sorry. I could kill myself if it would do any good! I wish you wouldn't take it so hard. I can't help it. You know it's impossible for people to make themselves love other people if they don't," cried Jo, softly patting his shoulder as she spoke.

"They do sometimes," came the muffled reply.

"I don't believe it's the right sort of love, and I'd rather not try it," said Jo.

"Don't tell me you love that professor you wrote to us about," said Laurie.

Jo wanted to laugh, but she stopped herself. "I haven't the least idea of loving him or anybody else," she said.

"But you will after a while, and then what will become of me?" Laurie moaned.

"You'll love someone else, too."

"I *can't* love anyone else, and I'll never forget you, Jo. Never, never!" he cried.

Laurie kept telling Jo how miserable he would be without her, until she couldn't stand listening to him anymore. "I shall always be very fond of you as a friend, but I'll never marry you. The sooner you believe it, the better for both us!" she said. Laurie turned sharply away. He went down to the river, got into his boat, and rowed away with all his might.

"When he comes back, he'll feel better," thought Jo. "And now I must go and prepare Mr. Laurence to be very kind to my poor boy. I wish he'd love Beth." Jo had a long talk with Mr. Laurence, who knew even better than Jo that love cannot be forced. When Laurie got back later that afternoon, Mr. Laurence suggested a trip abroad, just the two of them.

"I have business in London, and many friends in London and Paris. I'll visit them, and meanwhile you can go to Italy, Germany, Switzerland, and wherever you like." Laurie agreed to go, mainly to please his grandfather. Before much time had passed, they were off. As she watched them leave, Jo knew that the Laurie she once knew would never come back again.

10 *At Home and Abroad*

When Jo came home in June, she had been struck by the change in Beth. No one spoke of it or seemed aware of it, for it had come too slowly to startle those who saw her daily. But to Jo, the change was very clear. A heavy weight fell on Jo's heart as she saw her sister's face. There was a strange look about it, as if the mortal was slowly disappearing and the immortal was shining through with a pathetic beauty. Soon, that impression lost much of its power. Beth seemed happy and everyone seemed to think she was better.

After Laurie went away with his grandfather, the vague anxiety returned and haunted Jo. When Jo suggested the trip to the mountains that she had been saving for, Beth begged not to go so far away from home. They went to the seashore instead, where they spent all their time together. The people who lived there watched with sympathetic eyes the strong sister and the weak sister, who were always together. It seemed as if the sisters felt instinctively that a long separation was not far away.

They did feel it, yet neither spoke of it. Jo wondered if her sister really guessed the hard truth. One day, Beth whispered in Jo's ear, "I've known for a good while, Jo. I'm used to the idea now. Try not to be troubled about me, because it's best. It really is."

"Is this what made you so unhappy last fall, Beth?"

"Yes, I gave up hoping then, but I didn't want to admit it. But when I saw you all so well and strong, and full of happy plans, it was hard to feel that I could never be like you. Then, I was miserable, Jo."

"I thought that you loved Laurie, Beth," said Jo.

"How could I love Laurie, dear, when he was so fond of you?" asked Beth. "I do love him dearly, but he never could be anything to me but my brother. I hope he truly will be, sometime."

"Not through me, Beth. The only March sister left for him is Amy, and they would be a wonderful pair. But let's not talk about this now. I don't care what happens to anyone but you, Beth. You *must* get well."

"I want to, oh, so much! I try, but every day I get weaker. It can't be helped, Jo."

"It *shall* be helped," cried Jo, and she meant it.

"It can't," said Beth. "You will prepare Mother and Father for me, won't you? I've heard that the people who love best are often blindest to such things. Meg has John and the babies to comfort her, but you must help Mother and Father. Won't you, Jo?"

"If I can, Beth, but I won't give up yet."

"Jo, dear, I have a feeling that it never was intended I should live long. I'm not like the rest of you. I never made any plans about what I'd do when I grew up. I never thought of being married, as you all did. I couldn't seem to imagine myself as anything but stupid little Beth, trotting about at home, of no use anywhere but there. I never wanted to go away. The hardest part now is that I must leave all of you. I'm not afraid, but it seems as if I will be homesick for you even in heaven."

Jo could not speak. In that silent moment, she dedicated herself, soul and body, to Beth. When they got home, Jo could see that Mother and Father knew, too. Tired after her short journey, Beth went at once to bed, saying how glad she was to be at home.

When Jo came downstairs, she saw her father leaning his head on the mantel. He did not turn as she came in, and her mother stretched out her arms as if for help. Jo went to comfort her without speaking a word.

Meanwhile, in France, Amy was having a wonderful time. The best moment of all came when Laurie arrived at the Promenade des Anglais, a charming place in Nice[1], where all the fashionable people met to see and to be seen.

"Oh, Laurie, is it really you?" Amy said when she saw him. "I thought you'd never come!"

"I promised to spend Christmas with you. Here I am."

"How is your grandfather? When did you come? Where are you staying?"

"Very well—last night—at the Chauvain, to answer your questions. I called at your hotel, but you were out."

Amy and Laurie spent the rest of the afternoon catching up on news from home. As they talked, Amy watched Laurie, and she felt a new sort of shyness steal over her. He was changed, and she could not find the merry-faced boy she had left in the moody-looking man she was speaking to. He was handsomer than ever, she thought, but he looked tired and spiritless. Not sick, not exactly unhappy, but older and more serious than before.

A fancy Christmas party had been planned for that night. Amy invited Laurie to go with her and Aunt Carrol. It must be said that Amy did try to look her best that night. Time and absence had done their work on both the young people. Amy had seen her old friend in a new light, not as "our boy," but as a handsome and agreeable man. She was conscious of a very natu-

---

1. Nice a city in southeast France on the Mediterranean Sea

ral desire to find favor in his sight.

That evening, as Amy and Laurie danced, talked, and flirted, they were both aware that they were making new impressions on each other.

Back home, Meg was completely wrapped up in the duties of motherhood. Day and night she brooded over her babies with devotion and anxiety, often leaving John alone. John missed the wifely attentions he had been used to. But, since he adored his babies, he cheerfully gave up his comfort. He assumed that everything would be back to normal soon.

Three months passed, and nothing changed. Meg looked worn out and nervous, the babies took every minute of her time, and the house was neglected. When he got home after a long day at work, he was greeted by, "Hush! They just fell asleep."

The poor man was very uncomfortable. Home was merely a nursery. He was patient for six months, but when no signs of change appeared, he did what could only be expected. He tried to enjoy his evenings elsewhere. His friend Mr. Scott had married and was living nearby. John got in the habit of going over there for a few hours every evening. The parlor was always bright and attractive, the piano in tune, and supper set forth in tempting style.

John would have preferred his own fireside if it had not been so lonely. But since it was, he gratefully took the next best thing, and enjoyed his neighbor's society. Meg didn't mind at first. She found it a relief to know that John was having a good time. But after a few months, when the teething worries were over and the children went to sleep at regular times, she began to miss John.

"Yes," she would say, looking in the mirror, "I'm getting old and ugly. John doesn't find me interesting any longer. He leaves his faded wife and goes to see his pretty neighbor." She said nothing to anybody, however, until her mother found her in tears one day. When Marmee insisted on knowing what was wrong, Meg told her what had been happening. "If this goes on much longer, Marmee, I might as well be a widow. Men are very selfish, even the best of them."

"So are women. Don't blame John until you see where you are wrong yourself."

"But it can't be right for him to neglect me."

"Don't you neglect him?"

As usual, Marmee could see the problem clearly. "Talk with him, let him read to you, and exchange ideas. Most important of all, don't let John be a stranger to the babies."

Meg thought over what her mother had said, and acted upon it. A few days later, Meg had a good supper ready, dressed herself in pretty clothes, and put the children to bed early. At first John thought Meg might be expecting company. "No, John," she said, "I dressed up for a change."

"Well, it's delightful, and like old times," he told her.

The evening was very pleasant until the two children decided to get up. This time, however, John took over, and insisted that Daisy and Demi stay in bed. Both children threw tantrums, thinking they would get their mother to give in. But, remembering her mother's advice, Meg let John take care of the children.

Home grew homelike again, and John had no wish to leave it, unless he took Meg with him. This household happiness did not come all at once, but John and Meg had found the key to it. Each year of married life taught them how to use that key, unlocking the treasuries of real love and mutual helpfulness. These are things that the poorest may possess, and the richest cannot buy.

In Nice, Amy had begun to notice that Laurie didn't really spend his time doing anything. Amy, who always worked very hard at her art, was angry about this. Her earlier impressions of Laurie, as an attractive and accomplished young man, were quickly changing. "You have every chance to be good, useful, and happy," she said. "Instead, you are lazy, and miserable. You have been in Europe for nearly six months, and you've done nothing but waste time and money. Anyone can see that you are lovesick for Jo. If you want Jo to love you, you must do something splendid that will *make* her love you."

Laurie had nothing to say in his defense, for everything Amy said was true. The next day, Amy received a note from Laurie. "'Lazy Laurence' has gone to his grandpa, like the best of boys," he wrote. Even though Amy knew it was best for him to leave, she knew she would miss him.

11 Grieving and Growing

Though it brought them much sorrow, the family accepted Beth's illness and tried to bear it cheerfully. They put away their grief, and each did his or her part toward making her last year a happy one.

The most pleasant room in the house was set apart for Beth. In it was gathered everything that she most loved—flowers, pictures, her piano, and her cats. Father's best books found their way there, along with Mother's easy chair, Jo's desk, and Amy's finest sketches. Every day, Meg brought her babies to visit. John brought Beth the fruit she loved. Hannah cooked meals that Beth would enjoy. Amy sent little gifts and cheerful letters from across the sea.

The first few months were very happy ones. Beth often looked around at her family and said, "How beautiful this is!" It was good for everyone that this peaceful time was given to them as preparation for the sad hours to come. By and by, Beth found that talking was too tiring. Pain soon claimed her for its own. Ah, me! Such heavy days, such long, long nights, such aching hearts and pleading prayers. Those who loved her best were forced to see the thin hands stretched out to them and to hear the bitter cry, "Help me, help me!" But there was no way to help Beth in her sharp struggle with death.

Jo had never left her for an hour since Beth had said, "I feel stronger when you are here." Jo slept on a couch in the room, waking often to renew the fire or to wait on the patient creature who "tried not to be a trouble."

One night when Jo was asleep, Beth looked among the books on her table for something to read. Among the papers, she found a poem Jo had written. As she read it, she realized how much her sister loved her. Then the log in the fire broke apart, waking Jo. Beth said, with humble earnestness, "Jo, dear, I found this and read it. I knew you wouldn't mind. Do I mean all this to you?"

"Oh, Beth, so, so much!" Jo's head nestled next to her sister's.

"Then I don't feel as if I've wasted my life. I'm not as good as you say in the poem, but I have tried to do right. Now, it's too late to even try to do better. But it's such a comfort to know that someone loves me so much, and feels as if I've helped them. You must take my place here at home, Jo, and be everything to Father and Mother when I'm gone. Love is the only thing that we can carry with us when we go, and it makes the end so easy."

"I'll try, Beth," said Jo.

So the spring days came and went, and the birds came back in time to say good-bye to Beth. Seldom, except in books, do the dying say memorable words or see visions. Most often, the end comes as simply as sleep. In the dark hour before the dawn, Beth quietly drew her last breath, with no farewell but one loving look, one little sigh.

With tears and prayers and tender hands, her mother and sisters made her ready for the long sleep that pain would never disturb again. They felt that, to their darling Beth, death was a good angel.

When morning came, the room was very still. But a bird sang happily on a budding bough close by. The spring sunshine streamed in over the beloved face upon the pillow. Beth's face was so full of peace that those who loved her best smiled through their tears and thanked God that Beth was well at last.

Of course, news takes a long time to travel to Europe,[1] and Amy had no idea what was happening at home. She knew that Beth was not well, but the family thought it best not to let her know the details.

In London, Laurie was thinking about what Amy had said. He did not think he could make Jo love him, but he thought he might make her admire him. He resolved to do "something splendid" that would prove that her "No" had not spoiled his life. He decided to write a requiem[2] that would reach Jo's soul and melt every listener's heart.

Laurie went to Vienna, where he had some musical friends. He soon found that writing a requiem was beyond him. Often, in the middle of the saddest part, he would find himself humming a tune that reminded him of the Christmas party at Nice, when he was dancing with Amy.

Then he tried an opera, but again, he could not keep his mind on it. He wanted to make Jo his heroine, but he could only recall her oddities and faults. When he tried to invent another heroine, he found that she had golden hair and liked to dress in beautiful clothes. He made this vision his heroine. He got along fairly well with his opera until he grew bored with it. He started roaming about Vienna to get new ideas and refresh his mind. All through that winter, he realized a change was taking place.

He finally concluded that talent wasn't the same as genius. Realizing that he was not a musical genius, he

---

1. This was before the inventions of telephones or airplanes. Letters were sent across the Atlantic Ocean by boat.
2. **requiem** a solemn hymn for the dead

decided to tear up all the music he had written. Laurie began to wish that he had to work for a living. At least that would take up his time. He had thought that forgetting his love for Jo would take years. To his great surprise, he discovered it grew easier every day. He found himself thinking more about Amy, and he wrote her a letter. It was promptly answered, for Amy was homesick. Letters from Laurie made home feel closer. The letters flew back and forth, and by late spring, Laurie was hoping that Amy would ask him to return to Nice.

Amy, however, was having a problem of her own, and she didn't want Laurie around until she solved it. Fred Vaughn had finally asked her the question that she had once decided to answer with a "Yes." Now she said "No," for she had found that something more than money and position was needed to satisfy her heart's longing.

In May, Aunt Carrol and Amy went to Vevay³ to escape the heat in Nice. Perhaps for that reason, the letter telling Amy that Beth was failing never did reach her. When the letter about Beth's death arrived, the grass was already green above her sister's grave. The family thought that since it was too late to say good-bye to her sister, Amy should stay in Europe, and let absence soften her sorrow. Laurie got the news about Beth at about the same time Amy did, and he hurried to Amy's side.

The moment they saw each other, she dropped everything and ran to him. "Oh, Laurie, Laurie, I knew you'd come to me!" I think everything was said and settled then. Over the next few weeks, they enjoyed

---

3. **Vevay** a town in Switzerland on the northeast shore of Lake Geneva

each other's company. In spite of their sorrow, it was a happy time. One afternoon, while they were rowing on the lake, Amy said, "How well we pull together, don't we?"

"So well that I wish we might always pull in the same boat. Will you marry me, Amy?" asked Laurie very tenderly.

"Yes, Laurie," replied Amy in a very low voice.

Back at home, Jo was finding her promise to Beth very hard to keep. How could she "comfort Father and Mother," when her own heart ached for her sister? Poor Jo! These were dark days. Despair came over her when she thought of spending all her life in that quiet house.

When Marmee saw how grief-stricken Jo was, she tried to comfort her. The sympathy and love they all gave to one another was some help. Jo found that housework was not as distasteful as she had once thought, for she was reminded of Beth when she did it. She found herself humming the songs Beth used to hum. But Marmee and Father could see that Jo was not meant for such a life.

"Why don't you write?" suggested Marmee. "That always made you happy."

Even though she had no heart for it, Jo took her mother's advice. She sat at her desk and began scribbling out a story. Something got into that story that went straight to the hearts of those who read it. Against her wishes, her father sent it in to one of the popular magazines. To her surprise, it was not only paid for, but others were requested. For a small story, it was a great success, and she received many letters of praise for it.

"I don't understand it. What can there be in that little story to make people praise it so?" she asked her father.

"There is truth in it, Jo. That's the secret. You have found your style. You wrote with no thought of fame, and put your heart into it." So, taught by love and sorrow, Jo wrote her stories.

When Amy and Laurie wrote of their engagement, Mrs. March feared Jo's response. But though she was quiet at first, soon Jo was full of plans for "the children."

"You like the idea, Mother?"

"I hoped it would be so. Hints in her letters made me suspect that love and Laurie would win the day."

By and by, Jo roamed up into the attic. There stood four little wooden chests in a row, each marked with its owner's name and each filled with relics of the childhood and girlhood ended now and for all. Jo glanced into them. In her own, she saw a bundle of old exercise books. As she looked through them, she came across a message written in Professor Bhaer's hand. "Wait for me, my friend. I may be a little late, but I shall surely come," it said.

Jo thought, "Oh, if he only would! So kind, so good, so patient with me always, my dear old Fritz! I didn't value him half enough when I had him, but now how I should love to see him. Everyone seems to be going away from me, and I'm all alone." And holding the paper tightly, Jo began to cry. Was it self-pity, loneliness, or low spirits? Or was it the awakening of love? Who shall say?

Amy and Laurie returned home a few weeks later. To everyone's surprise, they had already gotten married. Laurie explained that Mr. Laurence had wanted to return home. Laurie couldn't let his grandfather travel alone, and he couldn't leave Amy behind. "So I just settled it by saying, 'Let's be married,'" Laurie said.

When Jo and Laurie were alone for a minute, he told her, "Jo, dear, I want to say one thing, and then we'll put it by forever. I shall never stop loving you, but that love has changed. I have learned to see I can share my love with sister Jo and wife Amy, and love you both dearly."

"We will be brother and sister and help one another all our lives, won't we, Laurie?" Jo said. Laurie took the hand she offered and laid his face on it for a moment.

What a wonderful reunion it was for the family! Mercy on us, how they did talk! First one, then the other, all trying to tell the story of three years in half an hour.

Jo watched the twins, and the joy of Amy and Laurie, and a sudden loneliness came strongly over her. Then there came a knock at the porch door. Jo went to answer it, and stared as if a ghost had come to surprise her. There stood a tall bearded gentleman, beaming on her from the darkness, like a midnight sun.

"Oh, Mr. Bhaer, I am so glad to see you!" cried Jo.

"And I to see Miss March. But you are having a party."

"No, it's just my family. Come in, and be one of us."

"Gladly," he said, as Jo led him inside.

"Father, Mother, this is my friend, Professor Bhaer," she said. Her face showed such pride and pleasure that she might as well have blown a trumpet.

Everyone greeted him kindly, for Jo's sake at first, but very soon they liked him for his own sake. Before long it was clear to everyone, even Jo, that Mr. Bhaer had come to court her. After he left, Jo sat by the fire for a few minutes with her mother and father.

"He seems like a wise man," said Mr. March.

"I know he is a good man," added Mrs. March.

"I thought you'd like him," was all Jo said.

12 *Happy Moments*

"What are you going to do with yourselves after you get settled?" Jo asked the newlyweds.

"We have our plans. We don't want to say much about them yet, but we won't be idle. I'm going into business and prove to Grandfather that I'm not spoiled. I'm tired of dawdling, and I mean to work like a man. And Amy will astonish you with her skill at giving parties and being an all-around good influence on the world. Isn't that right, dear?" asked Laurie, looking at Amy.

"Time will show," said Amy, putting on her gloves as they said good-bye.

"How happy those two seem together!" observed Mr. March, after they had left.

"Yes, and I think it will last," said Mrs. March.

"I know it will. I'm happy for Amy," said Jo. Then she smiled brightly as Professor Bhaer opened the gate with an impatient push.

Later in the evening, when Laurie and Amy were at home, Laurie said to his bride, "Amy, that man intends to marry our Jo!"

"I hope so, don't you, dear?"

"Well, my love, I think he's a fine fellow, but I do wish he was a little younger and a good deal richer."

"Now, Laurie, don't say that. If they love each other, it doesn't matter how old they are nor how poor. Women *never* should marry for money."

Amy caught herself up short as the words escaped her. She looked at her husband, who said:

"Certainly not, though you do hear charming girls

say that they intend to do it sometimes. If my memory serves me, you once thought it your duty to make a rich match. That accounts, perhaps, for your marrying a good-for-nothing like me."

"Oh, my dearest boy, hush! I forgot you were rich when I said 'Yes.' I'd have married you if you didn't have a penny, and I sometimes wish you were poor so that I could show how much I love you," said Amy. "It would break my heart if you didn't believe that I'd gladly pull in the same boat with you, even if you had to make your living by rowing on the lake."

"Of course I know that, darling. After all, you refused a richer man for me. You won't let me give you half the things I want to now," said Laurie.

"May I ask you a question, dear?"

"Of course you may."

"Will you care if Jo does marry Mr. Bhaer?"

"Oh, that's been bothering you, has it? Since I am the happiest man alive, I assure you I can dance at Jo's wedding with a heart as light as my heels. Do you doubt it, my darling?"

Amy looked up at him, and was satisfied. Her last little jealous fear had vanished forever. She thanked him, with a face full of love and confidence.

"I wish we could do something for that old professor. Couldn't we invent a rich uncle, who would leave him a tidy little fortune?" said Laurie.

"Jo would find out we had made it all up, and spoil it all. She is very proud of him. She said yesterday that she thought poverty was a beautiful thing."

"Bless her dear heart! She won't think so when she has a literary husband and a dozen little children to support. We won't interfere now, but we'll watch for our chance and help them when we can. I owe Jo for a part of my education, and she believes that people should pay their honest debts," said Amy.

"How delightful it is to be able to help others, isn't it?" said Laurie. "We'll do all kinds of good with our money. It's much better than keeping the money in the bank." So the young pair shook hands on it, and took a little walk around their garden. They felt that their hearts were more closely knit together by a love that could remember those less blessed than they.

While Laurie and Amy were taking little strolls over velvet carpets, Mr. Bhaer and Jo were enjoying strolls of a different sort. "I always take a walk toward evening," thought Jo, "and I don't know why I should give it up, just because I often happen to meet the professor along the way." It seemed that no matter which path she took, she was sure to meet the professor. He was either going to or returning from a visit to Meg's house, for he had grown very fond of the twins.

Under the circumstances, what could Jo do but greet him and invite him over for a visit? By the second week of this, everyone knew perfectly well what was going on. Yet everyone tried to look as if they were blind to the changes in Jo's face. They never asked why she sang as she worked, or did her hair three times a day, or got so flushed during her evening walk.

For two weeks, Mr. Bhaer came and went with loverlike regularity. Then he stayed away for three days.

"Disgusted, I guess, and gone home as suddenly as he came. It means nothing to me, of course, but I do think he could have come and said good-bye, like a gentleman," thought Jo, as she got ready for her walk.

"You'd better take the umbrella, dear. It looks like rain," said her mother, noticing that Jo was wearing her new bonnet.

"Yes, Marmee. Do you want anything in town? I've

got to run in and get some paper," said Jo.

"Yes, I need some needles. Will you be warm enough?"

"I believe so," said Jo.

"If you happen to meet Mr. Bhaer, bring him home to tea. I quite long to see the dear man," added Mrs. March. Jo made no answer, except to kiss her mother.

The stores where ladies bought needles were not down among the banks and warehouses, where gentleman were usually found. But somehow Jo found herself near there before she did a single errand.

Now she remembered the umbrella, which she had forgotten to take in her hurry to be off. As the raindrops came down faster, she thought, "It serves me right! What business did I have putting on all my best things to come down here, hoping to see the professor? Now I'll just have to forget about saving my bonnet, as I do my errands in the rain. It's no more than I deserve!"

Moments later, she found herself being sheltered by a somewhat shabby blue umbrella. Looking up, she saw Mr. Bhaer looking down. "What are you doing down here, my friend?" he asked.

"I'm shopping," said Jo. Mr. Bhaer smiled. He looked from the pickle factory on one side of the street to the leather factory on the other.

"You have no umbrella. May I go along, and carry your packages for you?"

"Yes, thank you," said Jo. In a minute she was walking away arm in arm with her professor, feeling as if the sun had suddenly come out and was more brilliant than ever.

"We thought you had gone," said Jo.

"Did you think I would go without saying good-bye to those who have been so kind to me?" he asked.

"No, *I* didn't. I knew you were busy, but we missed you—Mother and Father especially."

"And you?"

"I'm always glad to see you, sir."

In trying to keep her voice calm, Jo made it rather cool. The frosty "sir" at the end seemed to chill the professor. His smile vanished as he said, "I thank you, and I shall visit one more time before I go."

"You are going, then?"

"I no longer have any business here; it is done. I have been offered a teaching position in a college, where I will teach as I did at home in Germany. I will earn enough to make the way smooth for my two nephews. For this I should be grateful, don't you think?"

"Indeed I do. How splendid it will be for you to be doing what you like, and for me to see you often!"

"Ah, but we shall not meet often, I fear. I will be teaching out West."

"So far away!" said Jo, trying not to let her disappointment show.

Mr. Bhaer could read several languages, but he had not learned to read women yet. Jo's voice, face, and manner expressed half a dozen different moods in the course of half an hour. At first she had seemed delighted, then cool, then full of despair. He hardly knew what to think. But moments later, when Jo could not hide the tears that fell, Mr. Bhaer said, in a tender tone, "Heart's dearest, why do you cry?"

"Because you are going away," Jo sobbed.

"Oh, that is so good!" cried Mr. Bhaer. "Jo, I have nothing but much love to give you. I came to see if you could care for it. I waited to be sure that I was something more than a friend. Am I? Can you make a little place in your heart for old Fritz?"

"Oh, yes!" said Jo, as she folded both hands over his arm. She looked up at him with an expression that plainly showed how happy she would be to walk through life beside him.

Passers-by probably thought them a pair of harmless lunatics, for they strolled along happily in the deepening dusk and fog. They were enjoying the happy hour that seldom comes even once in any life, the magical moment that bestows youth on the old, beauty on the plain, wealth on the poor, and gives human hearts a taste of heaven.

By the time they had finished their little stroll, they had made their plans. They would be married in one year, after the professor had taught out West.

"I must help my nephews first, because I cannot break my word to my sister—not even for you. Can you forgive that, and be happy while we hope and wait?" he asked.

"Yes, I know I can, for we love each other, and that makes all the rest easy. The year will go fast."

"Ah, you give me such hope and courage, and I have nothing to give back but a full heart and these empty hands," said the professor.

Jo put both her hands in his, whispering tenderly, "Not empty now."

Over the next year, Jo and her professor worked and waited, hoped and loved. They met sometimes, and wrote many letters. At the end of the year, Aunt March died suddenly. When their first sorrow was over—for they loved the old lady in spite of her demanding ways—they found that they had cause for rejoicing. Aunt March had left her big house to Jo.

Jo and the professor were married soon after that. They turned the big house into a boarding school for boys. The rich people who sent their boys to Jo's school paid enough so that Jo was able to take in some poor boys who could not pay anything. Jo took care of them all like a mother, and Fritz was their teacher. Jo was a very happy woman there, in spite of hard work and constant noise. As the years went on, two little lads of her own came to increase her happiness. How they ever grew up in that whirlpool of boys was a mystery to their grandma and aunts, but they flourished like dandelions in spring.

On Marmee's 60th birthday, the whole family got together for an apple-picking party at Jo and Fritz's. The Marches, the Laurences, the Brookes, and the Bhaers turned out in full force, along with all the boys from the boarding school.

"I don't think I can call myself unlucky again, when my greatest wish has come true," said Jo, as she took her son's fist out of the milk pitcher.

"And yet your life is very different from the one you pictured long ago. Do you remember?" asked Amy.

"Yes, I remember, but the life I wanted then seems selfish, lonely, and cold to me now," Jo said. "I haven't given up the hope that I may write a good book, but I can wait."

"My dream was the most nearly realized," Meg said. "I asked for splendid things, but in my heart I knew I only wanted a little home, and John, and dear children."

"My dream is very different from what I planned, but I would not change it," said Amy, cradling her baby. "But I've begun to model a figure of a baby. Laurie says it's the best thing I've done."

"Anyone can see I'm far happier than I deserve," Jo said.

"Yes, Jo, I think your harvest will be a good one," said Mrs. March.

"Not half so good as yours, Marmee. We can never thank you enough for the patient sowing you have done," cried Jo.

"I hope there will be more wheat every year," Amy said softly.

"A large harvest, but I know there's room in your heart for it, Marmee dear," added Meg's tender voice.

Touched to the heart, Mrs. March could only stretch out her arms to gather children and grandchildren to herself. Then she said, with a voice full of love, "Oh, my girls, however long you may live, I never can wish you a greater happiness than this!"

REVIEWING YOUR READING

Chapter 1

FINDING THE MAIN IDEA

1. The best way to describe the March sisters is
   (A) shy (B) stingy (C) selfish (D) generous.

REMEMBERING DETAILS

2. The girls give _____ to the poor Hummel family
   (A) a Christmas tree (B) their breakfast (C) money
   (D) bread and milk

DRAWING CONCLUSIONS

3. The fact that Jo meets Laurie in the side room at the party suggests
   that Laurie is
   (A) shy (B) sick (C) rich (D) good-looking.

USING YOUR REASON

4. The reason Beth cannot take music lessons is that
   (A) she is too shy (B) she has no talent (C) she is ill (D) her
   family cannot afford them.

IDENTIFYING THE MOOD

5. The overall mood in the March home is one of
   (A) grief (B) love (C) worry (D) shame.

THINKING IT OVER

6. Meg seems to be more unhappy than her sisters at the fact that the
   family does not have much money. Why do you think it is more
   difficult for her?

Chapter 2

FINDING THE MAIN IDEA

1. The main idea of this chapter is that
   (A) the friendship between the Marches and the Laurences grows
   (B) Jo and Meg go to a play with Laurie (C) Amy burns Jo's book
   (D) Amy is punished at school.

REMEMBERING DETAILS

2. Amy asks Meg for money to buy

    (A) drawing pencils (B) an art book (C) pickled limes
    (D) sheet music.

DRAWING CONCLUSIONS

3. When Laurie says that he doesn't know anyone, we can assume that

    (A) he used to live elsewhere (B) he doesn't want to know anyone
    (C) he is hard to get along with (D) his grandfather doesn't let
    him have any friends.

USING YOUR REASON

4. Judging from the size of Mr. Laurence's personal library, we can
    assume that Mr. Laurence

    (A) never throws anything out (B) used to own a bookstore
    (C) likes to read (D) works in a public library.

THINKING IT OVER

5. Marmee tells Jo, "I feel anger nearly every day of my life. Think
    about Marmee's personality. What do you think would make her
    angry? Use evidence from the story to support your answer.

Chapter 3

FINDING THE MAIN IDEA

1. The main thing the girls learn from their week of playing and
    resting is that

    (A) work is just as important as play (B) everyone should have a
    cook (C) simple dinners are best (D) cream should be refrigerated.

REMEMBERING DETAILS

2. Laurie provided a _____ to be used as a post office.

    (A) basket (B) birdhouse (C) dollhouse (D) wagon

DRAWING CONCLUSIONS

3. The tightly laced dress Meg wears to the party must have been

    (A) too small for her (B) out of style (C) in style
    (D) inexpensive.

USING YOUR REASON

4. Laurie doesn't like Meg's new look because
   (A) she doesn't look like herself   (B) he is jealous   (C) he doesn't like blue silk   (D) he is too young to appreciate it.

IDENTIFYING THE MOOD

5. Jo's mood during her dinner party can be described as
   (A) proud   (B) pleased   (C) embarrassed   (D) hungry.

THINKING IT OVER

6. Why do you think Marmee encouraged the girls to try their experiment of not working for a week?

Chapter 4

FINDING THE MAIN IDEA

1. The most serious thing that happens in Chapter 4 is
   (A) the girls have a picnic   (B) Jo finishes a story   (C) Father gets ill   (D) Aunt March lends Marmee money.

REMEMBERING DETAILS

2. To get money for Marmee's trip, Jo
   (A) sold a story   (B) sold her hair   (C) got a job   (D) sold some of Amy's paintings.

DRAWING CONCLUSIONS

3. Jo's walking back and forth several times at the newspaper editor's office shows that she
   (A) needs exercise   (B) likes to walk   (C) is nervous   (D) doesn't know the right address.

IDENTIFYING THE MOOD

4. When the girls and Laurie talk about their plans for the future, the mood can be described as
   (A) serious   (B) hopeful   (C) depressed   (D) scared.

THINKING IT OVER

5. Why do you think Jo pretends to her family that she doesn't really care about her hair?

Chapter 5

FINDING THE MAIN IDEA

1. The biggest problem the family faces in Chapter 5 is
   (A) Mr. Brooke's interest in Meg (B) lack of money (C) Beth's illness (D) Hannah's bossiness.

REMEMBERING DETAILS

2. The disease Beth gets from the Hummel baby is
   (A) flu (B) pneumonia (C) measles (D) scarlet fever.

DRAWING CONCLUSIONS

3. When the doctor says that Mrs. March should be sent for, we can assume that
   (A) Beth is getting better (B) Beth is getting worse (C) he wants to be paid as soon as possible (D) Mr. March is getting better.

USING YOUR REASON

4. Scarlet fever was a more serious childhood illness in the 1860s than it is now because
   (A) people didn't know how to treat it (B) people were weaker then (C) the weather was warmer then (D) the weather was colder then.

IDENTIFYING THE MOOD

5. Just before Beth's fever turns, the mood in the room can best be described as
   (A) joyful (B) anxious (C) bored (D) excited.

THINKING IT OVER

6. Why do you think Amy is so eager to get home from Aunt March's?

Chapter 6

FINDING THE MAIN IDEA

1. The best Christmas surprise in Chapter 6 is
   (A) Jo and Laurie make a snow maiden (B) the plum pudding turns out (C) Mr. Laurence comes to visit (D) Father comes home.

REMEMBERING DETAILS

2. Meg and John plan to get married in

(A) a year   (B) six months   (C) three years   (D) a week.

DRAWING CONCLUSIONS

3. Mr. Laurence is angry with Laurie because

(A) he thinks Laurie offended the girls in some way   (B) Laurie won't keep his room clean   (C) Laurie won't do his homework (D) Laurie refuses to practice the piano.

USING YOUR REASON

4. Aunt March's biggest objection to the marriage between Meg and John Brooke is that

(A) John is not educated   (B) John has no manners   (C) John is too poor   (D) Meg is too young.

IDENTIFYING THE MOOD

5. Laurie's mood after the argument with his grandfather can best be described as

(A) busy   (B) worried   (C) thankful   (D) angry.

THINKING IT OVER

6. Why do you think Aunt March said to Meg, "If you marry that poor tutor, not one penny of my money will go to you"? What can you tell about Aunt March by this?

Chapter 7

FINDING THE MAIN IDEA

1. The biggest change in Meg's life is that she

(A) goes to college   (B) marries John   (C) gets scarlet fever (D) takes up oil painting.

REMEMBERING DETAILS

2. Amy's luncheon party was ruined because of

(A) loud guests   (B) guests not attending   (C) burned food (D) Beth's illness.

DRAWING CONCLUSIONS

3. We can assume that Laurie's friends sighed about Amy because she is

   (A) charming and pretty   (B) a tomboy   (C) an artist   (D) a good chess player.

USING YOUR REASON

4. The reason Meg and John do not take a honeymoon trip is that
   (A) Meg does not like to travel   (B) they cannot afford it
   (C) Meg does not want to leave Marmee   (D) John cannot get the time off work.

THINKING IT OVER

5. Why do you think Amy wanted to have a luncheon party for the girls in her drawing class? Use evidence from the story to support your answer.

Chapter 8

FINDING THE MAIN IDEA

1. Jo's biggest disappointment in Chapter 8 is that
   (A) Aunt Carrol invites Amy, not Jo, to go to Europe   (B) Amy criticizes her social skills   (C) she doesn't sell any stories   (D) her best dress gets mud on it.

REMEMBERING DETAILS

2. Meg's twin babies are nicknamed
   (A) Laurie and Carrol   (B) Jack and Jill   (C) Tigger and Roo
   (D) Daisy and Demi.

DRAWING CONCLUSIONS

3. Amy seems to think that the most important thing to look for in a husband is
   (A) good looks   (B) a sense of humor   (C) kindness   (D) money.

USING YOUR REASON

4. The reason John cannot afford his new coat is that
   (A) he has lost his job   (B) the babies cost too much   (C) Meg has spent the money on silk   (D) he has lost the money playing cards.

THINKING IT OVER

5. Why do you think Aunt Carrol chose Amy instead of Jo as a companion for her trip to Europe?

Chapter 9

FINDING THE MAIN IDEA

1. Laurie's greatest disappointment is that
(A) Beth does not love him (B) Jo will not marry him (C) Jo moves to New York (D) he can't sell any stories.

REMEMBERING DETAILS

2. Jo meets Mr. Bhaer at
(A) a poetry reading (B) the boardinghouse where they both live (C) a night class (D) a party.

DRAWING CONCLUSIONS

3. From Jo's description of the way Mr. Bhaer plays with the children, we can assume that
(A) he is being paid for it (B) he likes children (C) he is a foolish old man (D) he is doing it for the exercise.

USING YOUR REASON

4. The reason that Jo won't marry Laurie is that
(A) she thinks of him as a brother (B) he is not rich enough (C) he is not smart enough (D) she thinks that Laurie loves Beth.

THINKING IT OVER

5. What special qualities does Professor Bhaer have that cause Jo to value her friendship with him? Use evidence from the story to support your answer.

Chapter 10

FINDING THE MAIN IDEA

1. Marmee's advice to Meg is
(A) not to neglect John as she cares for the babies (B) to learn how to make jelly (C) always wear pretty clothes (D) to keep a clean house.

REMEMBERING DETAILS

2. Laurie comes to visit Amy in

    (A) London (B) Heidelberg (C) Vienna (D) Nice.

DRAWING CONCLUSIONS

3. Based on what Beth says to Jo, we can guess that she knows

    (A) she will soon be well (B) she is dying (C) Jo has been writing trashy stories (D) Laurie is sad.

USING YOUR REASON

4. The reason John spends his evenings at the Scotts' is that

    (A) Meg is not a good cook (B) the Scotts have a better piano (C) Meg seems too busy to pay attention to him (D) the children are too noisy for him.

THINKING IT OVER

5. Think about Marmee's advice to Meg about her relationship with John. Explain why you do or do not agree with Marmee.

Chapter 11

FINDING THE MAIN IDEA

1. The most important thing that happens in Chapter 11 is that

    (A) Laurie tries to write an opera (B) Beth dies (C) Beth finds a poem Jo had written (D) Laurie keeps thinking of Amy.

REMEMBERING DETAILS

2. Laurie asks Amy to marry him while they are

    (A) having dinner (B) dancing (C) listening to music (D) rowing on the lake.

DRAWING CONCLUSIONS

3. Laurie finds it easier than he had expected to get over his love for Jo because

    (A) he is falling in love with Amy (B) he is angry with Jo (C) he is far away from Jo (D) he had never really loved Jo in the first place.

THINKING IT OVER

4. Why is Jo so happy to see Mr. Bhaer? Find evidence in the story to support your answer.

Chapter 12

FINDING THE MAIN IDEA

1. The main thing Jo does in Chapter 12 is
   (A) walk in the rain   (B) marry Mr. Bhaer   (C) write letters to Mr. Bhaer   (D) have an apple-picking party.

REMEMBERING DETAILS

2. Aunt March surprises Jo by
   (A) buying her a ticket to Europe   (B) sending her to college
   (C) adopting some children   (D) leaving her house to Jo.

DRAWING CONCLUSIONS

3. When Amy says that she owes Jo for a part of her education, she is referring to the fact that
   (A) she and not Jo, who was older, had been chosen to go to Europe   (B) Jo sent her some money   (C) Jo bought her art supplies   (D) Jo read books to her.

THINKING IT OVER

5. Why did Jo say that Mr. Bhaer's hands were "not empty now"?